Tonbridge's Industrial Heritage

Tonbridge's Industrial Heritage

A guide and gazetteer

edited by Anthony Wilson

with contributions by Christopher Chalklin,
Frank Tullett, Ian Goodacre, Peter Swan,
Margaret Wilson and Anthony Wilson

Tonbridge Historical Society

Copyright © The editor and contributors, 2005

All rights reserved. No part of this publication may be reproduced, stored in a retrieval system, or transmitted in any form or by any means, electronic, mechanical, photocopying, recording or otherwise, without the prior permission of the publisher.

ISBN 0 9523563 2 5

Set in 11.5-point and 10-point Joanna using WordPerfect and Pagemaker software.

Printed in Tonbridge by Pica Press.

Published by Tonbridge Historical Society, 8 Woodview Crescent, Hildenborough, Tonbridge, Kent TN11 9HD. E-mail: ths@clementi.demon.co.uk

Contents

Acknowledgments		7
Maps of Sites, and Note on Gazetteer Entries		8
Introduction		11
Tonbridge Foundations: topography and geology – *Frank Tullett*		13
Tonbridge Town: a brief historical survey – *Christopher Chalklin*		17
Guide and Gazetteer:		
A	Agriculture and allied trades	23
B	Water and wind power	32
C	Extractive industry	38
D	Metalworking and engineering	47
E	Manufacturing	50
F	Utilities and services	62
G	Communications and entertainment	74
H	Transport	81
Principal sources		95
List of subscribers		97
Index		99

Acknowledgments

Many people have helped in the preparation of this book and in the research that has gone into it. In particular we would like to thank the staff of Tonbridge Reference Library, the Centre for Kentish Studies in Maidstone, the Science Museum Library and the Templeman Library at the University of Kent.

For access to individual sites, or information about them, we are grateful to Mr and Mrs Barham (Old Mill Cottage, Tonbridge), David Cufley (ed. *Brickmakers' Index*), Dennis Goodland (Goodland Engineering), Anne Hughes (Hadlow Historical Society), Diane Huntingford (Somerhill), Richard Johnson (Lower Haysden), Paul W. Sowan (Croydon Natural History and Scientific Society), Mr J. R. Thickett (former manager of Quarry Hill Brickworks), Duncan Welch (R. Allen Ltd), and to staff at the following organisations: The British Brick Society, The Environment Agency, GlaxoSmithKline (Leigh), The Gunpowder Mills Study Group, The Kent Underground Research Group, R.M.C. (Aggregates) Southern, Ltd (Postern Works, Tonbridge), South-East Water plc (Pembury), Southern Water Services (Tonbridge Waste Water Treatment Works), Tonbridge and Malling Borough Council (Planning and Engineering Services), The Upper and Lower Medway Internal Drainage Boards, Wallace and Tiernan plc (Tonbridge), and The Wealden Iron Research Group.

The editor would particularly like to thank Christopher Chalklin, Pat Hopcroft, Brian Meyers and Sydney Simmons, who read the book in proof and suggested many helpful corrections and improvements. He is grateful also to Shiela Broomfield (Secretary) and the committee of Tonbridge Historical Society, to Pat Hopcroft for help with the photographs, to his wife Margaret for much practical help and support, and, of course, to the contributors themselves. Remaining errors and omissions in the text are the responsibility of the editor. He and the contributors would be glad to be told of any errors, and to receive further information readers may have about any of the sites.

Geological information in the map on page 15 is reproduced by permission of the British Geological Survey (© NERC; all rights reserved; IPR/67-40C). Other maps are reproduced from out-of-copyright Ordnance Survey editions, with the addition of newer roads where appropriate. Maps accompanying gazetteer entries are from the O.S. 25-inch series of Kent, sheets L(50)/11 2nd ed. (entry B4), L(50)/12 3rd ed. (C11), L(50)/16 1st ed. (C15), L(50)/15 3rd ed. (C16), and L(50)/4 2nd ed. (C20).

Photographs

Photographs credited to 'THS' are from the photographic or archive collections of Tonbridge Historical Society, held in Tonbridge Reference Library. Photographs not otherwise credited are by the editor. The photographs on pages 56 and 61 are reproduced by permission of the Kent and East Sussex Courier.

Maps of sites and key to gazetteer entries

Maps on these two pages show sites relating to Agriculture and allied trades (Section A), Metalworking and engineering (D), Manufacturing (E), Utilities and services (F), Communications and entertainment (G) and Transport (H).

For sites relating to Water and wind power (Section B), see the map on page 13.
For sites relating to Extractive industry (C), see the map on page 15.

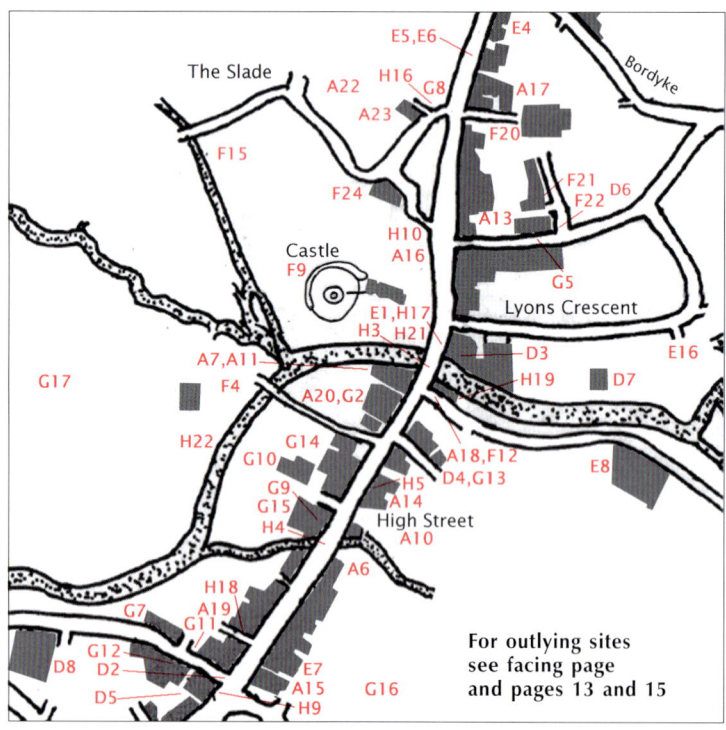

Sites in the town centre

Gazetteer entries

Each entry carries one of the following symbols:
- ★ something remains, either in a public place or visible from a public place
- ☆ something remains, but not visible from a public place
- • nothing found
- − site not inspected.

Six-figure national grid references are given for all sites, apart from a few which are small or hard to locate, which have eight-figure references. All should be preceded by the letters 'TQ'. The abbreviation 'O.S.' stands for 'Ordnance Survey'.

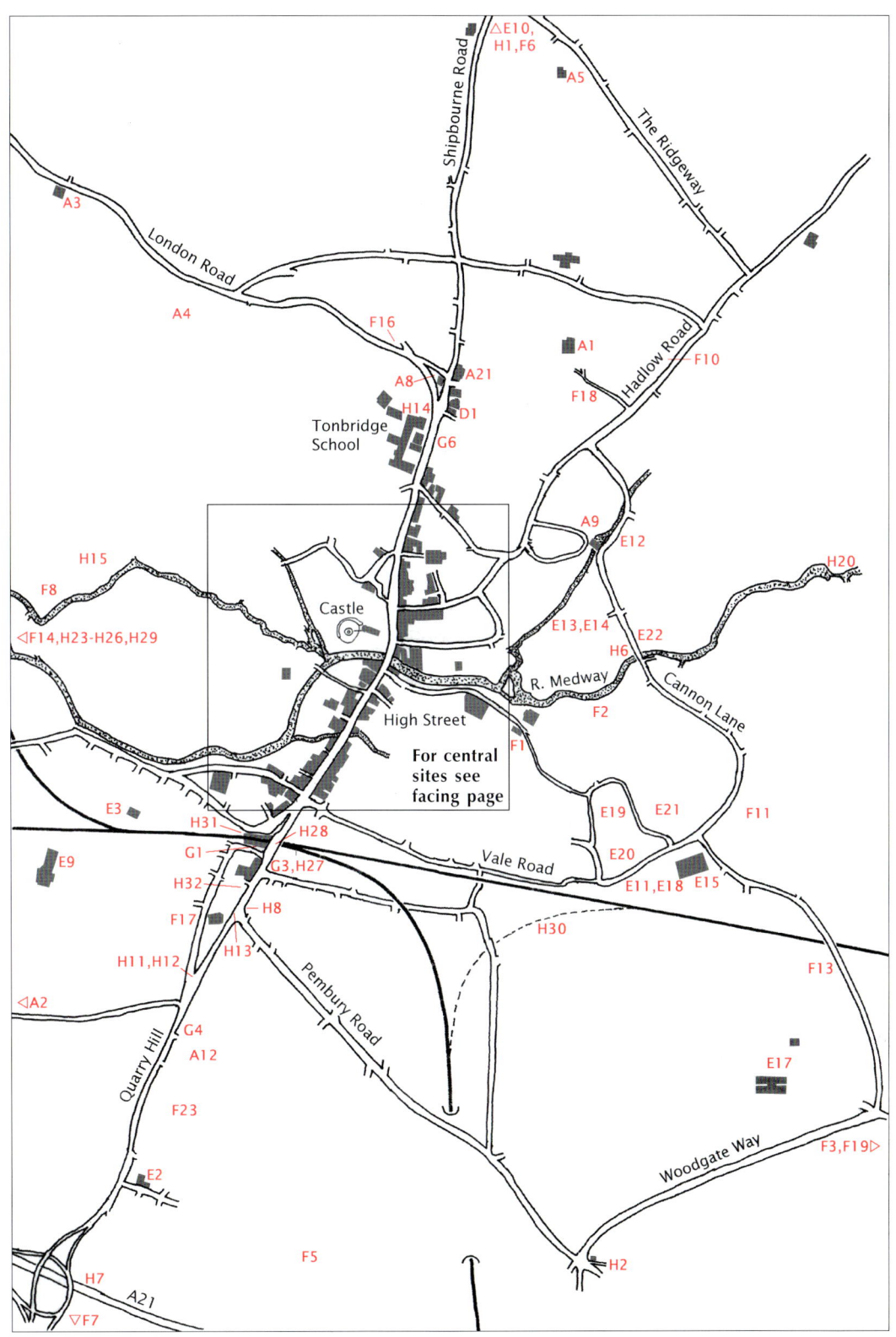

Sites in outlying areas

Introduction

Many British towns have been notable in the past for particular industries – straw hats from Luton and pencils from Keswick, for example – and Tonbridge is no exception. At various times in its past the town has been noted in Directories for the production of the wooden items known as Tunbridge Ware, for its cricket ball industry, for the manufacture of gunpowder, and more recently as a centre for printing. But these are only a small part of the town's industrial heritage; just as significant in the long term have been the changes that were not specific to the town, but in which Tonbridge and its citizens participated as part of the wider process of industrialisation that has transformed the country in the last two and a half centuries. One consequence was improved communications, principally in the form of water and rail transport and better roads, and the new technologies of the telegraph and telephone. Another was the surge in brick-making that changed the look, and the size, of the town. A third was the better living and working conditions brought by a sewerage system, a piped water supply, and gas and electricity.

In addition, throughout its history apart from recent years, Tonbridge, as an important market town and population centre for the western Weald, has served the needs of agriculture in the area, and been involved at various times with the Wealden cloth and iron-making industries.

This book is a product of the 'Industrial Survey' undertaken by a group of members of Tonbridge Historical Society. Its purpose was to locate, record and investigate all surviving signs of the town's industrial history and development, using maps and published documents and archives, and by scrutinising the actual sites. The result is a Gazetteer of 98 sites at which something, however meagre, still remains to be seen. Also included are a further 66 sites once relevant to the town's industrial development, but now completely vanished. The Gazetteer entries form the major part of the book, and are grouped under eight headings: agriculture, water and wind power, extractive industry, metalworking and engineering, manufacturing, utilities and services, communications, and transport. In addition to listing sites, each section includes a brief historical summary. To complete the picture, general introductory chapters have been included to give an outline of the geology and topography of the area, and of the broad historical development of the town.

The project proved to be an ambitious one – much more so than anticipated when we began – and limits had to be set. Geographically we have concentrated on the area that was once the domain of Tonbridge Urban District Council, shown in outline on the map on page 15, though we have strayed outside where it seemed appropriate, particularly in dealing with water-powered sites and with brick-making.

To cover the much larger area of the earlier Tonbridge Parish, or the later Tonbridge and Malling District, would have extended the task beyond our means. In dealing with manufacturing industry we have followed earlier practice by taking the term to include only those enterprises whose products served national, or even international, markets, rather than simply meeting local needs. Mainly excluded are the numerous bakers, dressmakers, saddlers, shoemakers, tailors, and other tradespeople whose products were often made at High Street premises and sold only within the town. Historically we have not been able to give detailed attention to developments in the later 20th century, particularly those occurring on the industrial estates, where enterprises have become too numerous and sometimes too ephemeral to record in this Survey. A separate project to cover more recent developments would be useful.

For convenience we have adopted the spelling 'Tonbridge' throughout the book, even when dealing with times when 'Tunbridge' would have been a more usual rendering. Measures of size and distance are given in imperial units rather than metric, this seeming more appropriate in a historical study. To a fair approximation, one yard (3 feet) is the same as one metre, and one mile is 1.6 kilometres.

We hope that local readers of this book will be encouraged to seek out surviving relics of Tonbridge's industrial past – or perhaps become aware for the first time of the significance of things they pass in their everyday lives but have hitherto taken for granted. Beyond this, we believe the book will be of interest to anyone with a general interest in the historical development of English towns. Tonbridge is *typical* rather than *special* in its industrial history, a useful exemplar in studying the effects of industrialisation in Britain. What happened here also occurred in much the same way and at much the same times in numerous other places.

The importance of a record of the type represented by this book has increased even in the time since we began our Survey. The policy of in-filling, in which existing sites within the town are favoured for redevelopment over new sites in outlying areas, places former industrial locations under particular threat. A number of historical sites in the town have already been obliterated by new development, not least the former Whitefriars Press buildings, and the market area and nearby Capitol Cinema. More sites will surely move from the 'something visible' category to the 'nothing now remains' category in the years ahead. What is presented here is a snapshot of a fading scene, and the words 'now' or 'currently' where they appear in these pages must be taken to mean 'in the summer of 2005'.

Anthony Wilson
September 2005

Tonbridge Foundations: topography and geology

Frank Tullett

Both topography and geology can be shown to have had some effect on the location of industry and services in Tonbridge. The topography or relief is ultimately mainly the result of dissection by rivers, and is shown, with drainage, in the map below. Some local names which relate to topographical features are added to the map. The geological background, which is to a considerable degree reflected in the topography, is shown in a somewhat simplified form in the map on page 15.

Tonbridge developed at an important crossing point on the River Medway, where

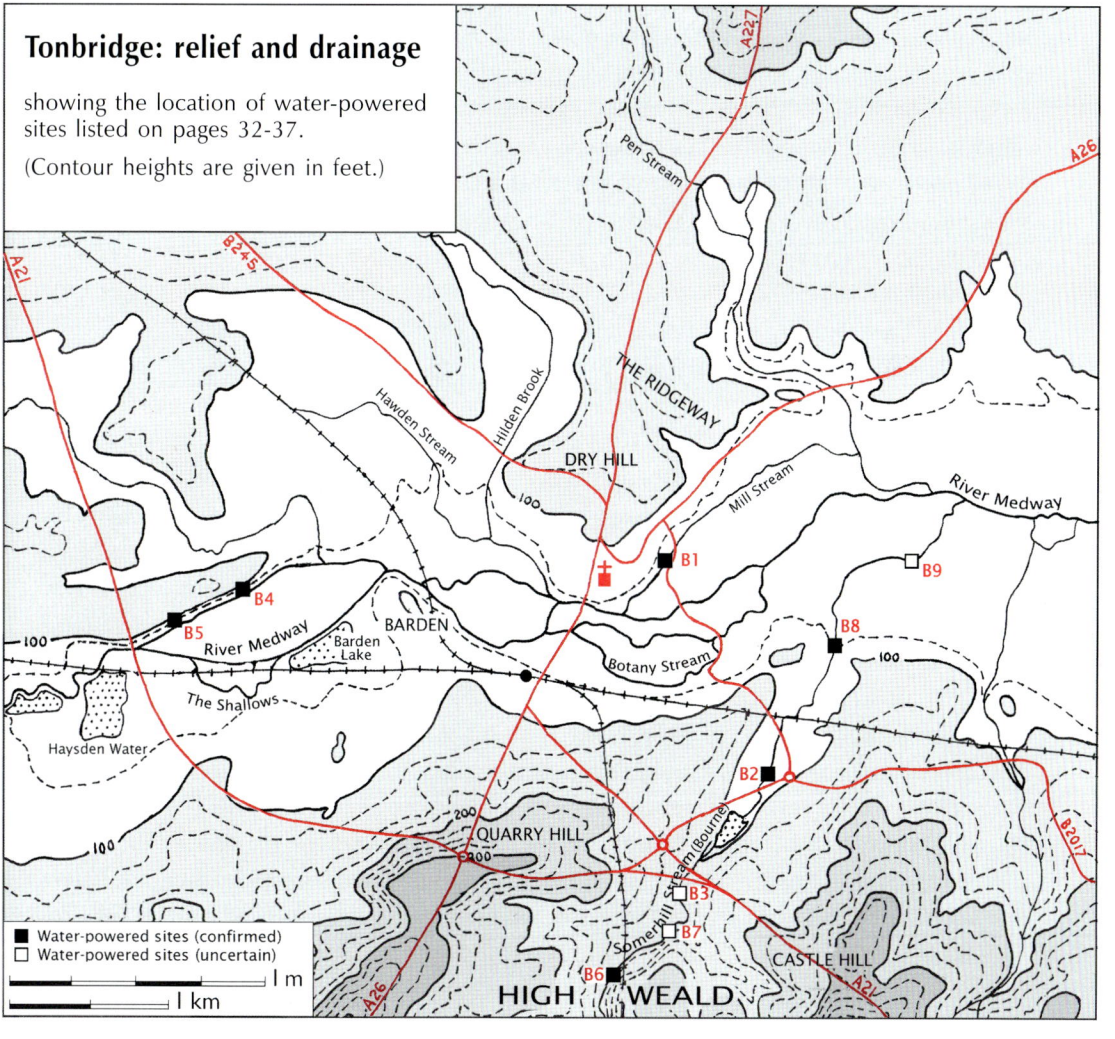

Tonbridge: relief and drainage

showing the location of water-powered sites listed on pages 32-37.

(Contour heights are given in feet.)

the flood plain narrows to barely a mile in width. Both above and below the town this well-watered land is much wider, and in effect the drainage of the upper valley is funnelled towards Tonbridge. The river is here flowing in its lower course, with a tendency for the channel to break up naturally into innumerable branches, these now much affected by man's activities. Across the urban area the fall of the Medway is very slight, but the river is described as having a 'flashy' regime in its natural unregulated state, meaning that water levels rise and fall rapidly following heavy rain in the upper catchment area. This has led to a need for much river control locally and nowadays the Medway is reputedly one of the most heavily regulated rivers for its size in England.

Clearly, physical features have been of importance in the growth and development of Tonbridge, the most salient of these being the presence of a major river and its flood-plain. The Medway Valley lies astride the direct and important early route from London to Rye. Locally a spur of higher and firmer land projects southwards, and as a result the flood-plain is much narrower here than elsewhere, so providing a more convenient crossing-point at Tonbridge. The Castle and town developed on this hillside above the river, and the low-lying flood plain above and below the town remained, until quite recently, a negative area for development. In time other routes converged on this river crossing, emphasising the nodality of the town. Centuries later the canalisation of the Medway and the construction of the early main-line railway from London to Dover would further the importance of Tonbridge as a Central Place.

In later times some growth took place on the level land between the river and the rising land of Quarry Hill to the south. This area has until recently been prone to flooding, being formerly crossed by no fewer than five water-courses. In modern times Tonbridge has developed the so-called 'dumb-bell' shape typical of towns located on lowland rivers, with development fanning out on the higher land away from the flood-plain to north and south. (A similar form is shown by Godalming on the River Wey in Surrey.)

Despite its shallow fall, the River Medway and its tributaries have provided water power at several sites (see gazetteer entries B1-B9), most notably at the former Leigh Powder Mills (B4) where local topography facilitated the construction of numerous parallel water-driven mills. To the east of the town the water-powered Town Mill provided a nucleus around which manufacturing industry began to develop in the early 20th century, but unlike in some other river valleys no large-scale industry has developed here consequent on the available water-power. Despite the continual risk of flooding, much of the town's early industrial development was along the banks of the Medway, mainly between the Great Bridge and the Postern area, and also alongside the Botany stream. For some riverside concerns such as the gas and electricity works (pages 62 and 69) the river was a means of transporting raw materials rather than a source of power, and for others, such as the tanneries, it was the availability of water itself that was the attraction. The natural easterly drainage of the area also facilitated the construction of the main sewage works downstream of the town (F11), from which effluent can pass into the river. Some low-lying areas in the urban area do, however, need small sewage pumping stations to elevate the flow so that it can proceed by gravity to the works.

Tonbridge Foundations: topography and geology

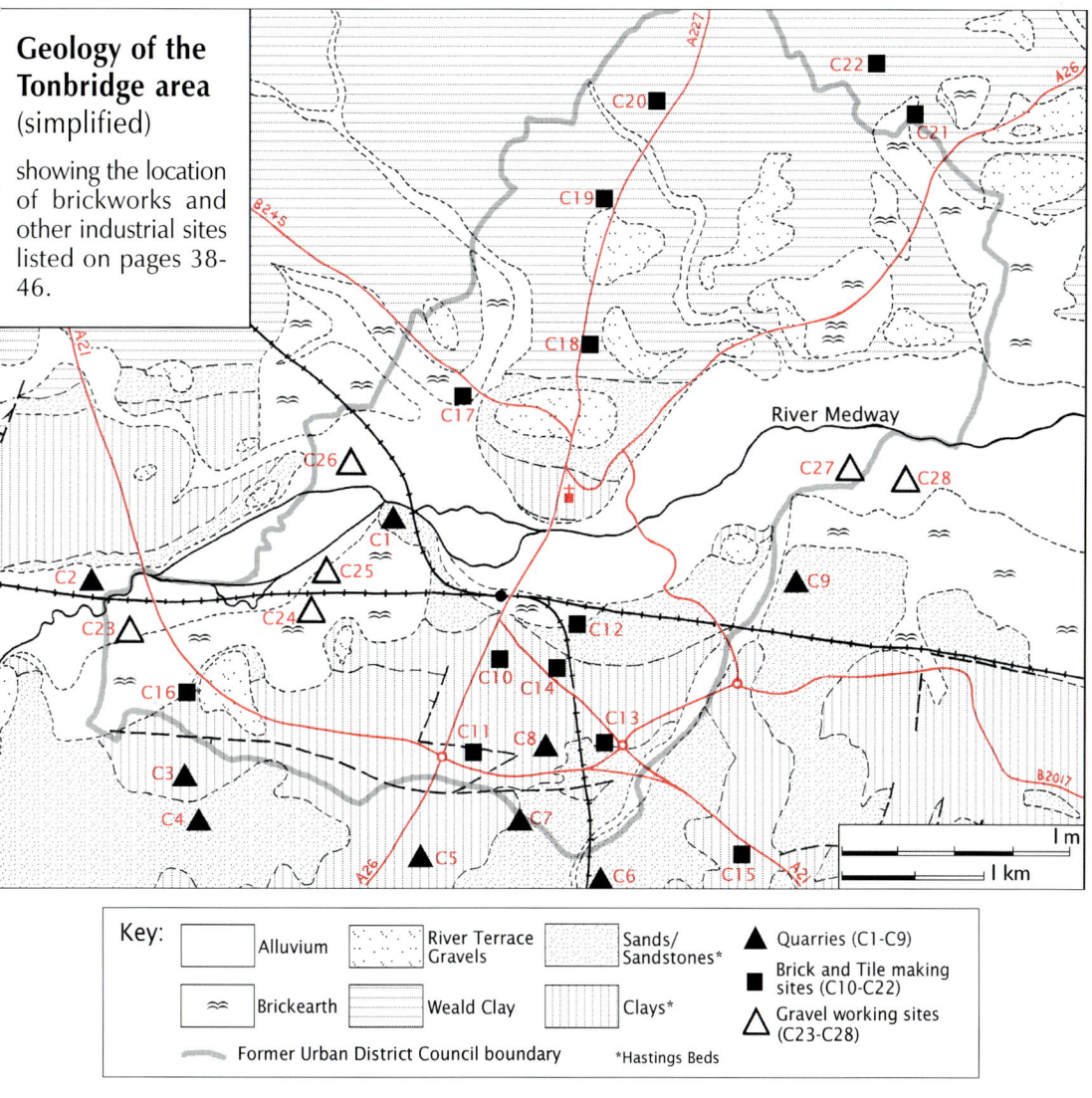

Geologically, the 'solid' rocks of the Tonbridge area consist of varied strata belonging to the Cretaceous System (135-65 million years before present) which dip at a very low angle towards the north. These tilted beds form part of the northern limb of the Wealden upfold or anticline, the major surface structure of south-eastern England, a consequence of pressures emanating during the Alpine Orogeny or mountain-building episode of Tertiary times. Through geological ages this fold has been slowly eroded and the more resistant strata now stand out as higher land. Two major formations outcrop in the Tonbridge area: in the north the Weald Clay is associated mainly with lower relief, whereas to the south of the Medway the sandstones and clays of the Hastings Beds give rise to the undulating country of the High Weald.

Over considerable areas these strata are overlain by geologically superficial deposits often known as 'Drift' which bear little or no relation to the underlying rocks and frequently have a strong connection with the drainage of the district. Recent alluvium fills most of the river valleys, and River Gravels at higher levels (Terrace Gravels) reflect the history of denudation. Deposits of so-called Brickearth have a somewhat problematic origin. Usually a fine and structureless loamy material, it may have originated as a wind-blown deposit during periglacial times, but here it seems to have been reworked as an alluvial deposit.

The rocks of this area have at times provided useful materials, and still support extractive industry. It is likely that the sandstones of the Hastings Beds have been quarried on a small scale from earliest times for local constructional work, and in mediaeval times they certainly provided good building-stone for important local buildings such as the castle and church. During the 16th and 17th centuries, and probably much earlier, deposits of clay-ironstone in the same beds supported a local iron-smelting and working industry, part of the formerly important Wealden iron industry (see B6-B9). From the 18th century onward the various clay strata and the brickearth deposits became important in the growth of numerous brick and tile manufacturing sites, opened up as the town developed (C10-C22). Gravel working in the Medway valley is the only extractive industry still in operation (C23-C28) and even this activity should cease in a few years.

River gravels filtered the early public water supply, and still today some supply is obtained from this source (page 64). However, most of the demand has been met from deep boreholes into various aquifers, at present from strata underlying the Sevenoaks area. Water is pumped to various high-level reservoirs from where a gravitational distribution system is possible, illustrating another effect of local relief. A water tower formerly stood at a commanding point on the Pembury Road.

Drainage has presented serious problems for the later growth of the town which has impinged on the flood-plain to a considerable degree. Much of the present town centre is so situated and flooding has occurred many times, but with the construction of the Leigh Barrier in recent years (F14) such events are now unlikely to recur.

Tonbridge Town: a brief historical survey

Christopher Chalklin

Tonbridge was an unincorporated town lying in the largest parish in Kent before the mid-nineteenth century. Almost from the Norman Conquest there was a considerable settlement. It lay on a main road from London to Hastings, Rye and Winchelsea, on the only important river crossing, that of the Medway. During the reign of William I this road became a principal route to Normandy. To protect it a castle was built at Tonbridge, the town arising near its walls. Its strategic position made it a natural centre for the neighbouring villages, so that by the beginning of the 14th century its few hundred inhabitants were serving the surrounding area with a market, craftsmen and tradesmen.

From the bank of the northernmost branch of the Medway the land rises gently northwards, forming a well-drained site for the town. The ground determined that it should lie along a single highway until the 1840s and 1850s, and not at the junction of several roads. The main road from Rye joined another highway from Sussex some 200 yards to the south of the Medway, so as to use a single river crossing. Further, as the clay, sand and gravel on which the town lies are bounded on the west side for nearly half a mile north of the River by low lying alluvial ground, the London road from the west joined the road from due north about half a mile north of the old market place in the town centre. Between this junction and the River only one lateral road, from Maidstone to the east, enters the High Street.

Until the 19th century houses were contiguous for 200 or 300 yards from the river up the High Street; then they were well spaced, surrounded by gardens, orchards and closes, until they reached the junction with the London road. A few other buildings lay in the two streets leading off the market place. To the south of the main bridge the low lying land was frequently flooded, preventing extensive building, so that there were only a few houses as far south as the junction of the Rye and Frant roads, nearly three-quarters of a mile from the top of the town.

Down to the early 18th century houses were of timber-framed structure, surviving examples being of two and occasionally three storeys. Only the Castle (occupied until 1646), the Church and the School (built in the 1550s) were stone. Brick building began in the early 18th century, as wood grew scarcer. The fashion for brick facades spread from north Kent as the better temperature and cleanliness, and the reduction of fire risk became more appreciated.

In the 16th century and until the 1640s the population may have grown by at least 50 per cent. On the first date at which there is firm evidence, in 1664, there were 141 households, suggesting about 600 people. The trades and crafts were simple, suggesting a lack of specialisation, being dominated by butchers, shoemakers and tailors. Further modest growth of long-distance road traffic and local trade increased the population to about 900 by 1739.

The town began to be transformed after the river was made navigable upstream from Maidstone to Tonbridge in the 1740s. As the hub of the road system of the western Weald, the town became the 'port' on the upper part of the river. The barges took agricultural produce, hops, and timber down to Maidstone, Chatham and London, and brought back coal, lime, and imported softwoods. The topographer Hasted wrote in 1792 that 'as a result of the navigation the trade of the town has greatly increased'. Road traffic increased as Hastings and especially Tunbridge Wells grew. The coaches waiting daily outside the Rose & Crown Inn were almost as much a symbol of the town's new prosperity as were the spacious wharf on the south bank of the Medway, and the long queue of wagons in the hop-picking season stretching from the river up to the Market Place.

By 1841 the population reached 3,115, having more than trebled in the last century. In 1664 Tonbridge was a small and obscure market town, with the neighbouring towns of Westerham, Sevenoaks and Cranbrook all larger. In 1841 Tonbridge was three times the size of Westerham, twice the size of Cranbrook and a little larger than Sevenoaks.

The face of the town was transformed by bricks. By 1730 two mansions had been erected almost opposite each other at the top of the town by two local landowners. Along the High Street substantial brick inns, shops and houses appeared one after the other. In 1775 the main bridge was rebuilt, and in 1798 a Town Hall was put up in the market place by the lord of the manor. Yet the change had its darker side. By 1840 there were at least half a dozen groups of jerry-built terraced cottages in tightly packed rows in alleys off the high street, occupied by the lower classes. Those at the south end of the town had sewers which were just open ditches joined to the sluggish southernmost branch of the Medway. Insanitary conditions brought periodic outbreaks of Asiatic cholera and smallpox by the 1840s, especially in this area.

Although nonconformist churches appeared in Tonbridge town and Tunbridge Wells before 1830, Tonbridge Parish Church was the only Anglican place of worship apart from King Charles Church (which did not conduct marriages or burials) at the extreme south end of the parish. Until 1835 parish relief was administered by the overseers of the poor from the town under the general control of the Vestry, with the workhouse in the tiny Bank Street between the Castle and the High Street. The Vestry also handled highway repairs through its surveyors, and other civil as well as church matters, all paid for by parish rates. On the other hand the economic and social gulf between the town and the rural part of the parish widened with the growth of its inhabitants. All but a very few of the substantial tradesmen and professional men had ceased to gain any livelihood directly from the land by the mid-19th century. Trades were more varied than formerly, reflecting both the increased specialisation one would expect from larger numbers, and an improved standard of living among the middle class. The clothing trades now included drapers, milliners, dressmakers, bonnet makers and hatter, while among those selling food and drink were fishmongers, milkmen, confectioners, tea dealers and a wine merchant.

Except for a small Tunbridge-ware factory on the north bank of the Medway, there were only agricultural industries like the brewery, a tannery, and corn mill. All these indirectly linked the town to the countryside in that they used materials produced on Kentish farms. The brewery, tannery and mill lay beside or near the river to use its water, the two latter works lying just to the east of the town, close to the road to Maidstone. The existence of any windmills on higher land before the 1840s is unknown, as is the location of the earlier brickworks.

The town's dominance of the parish almost disappeared between 1841 and 1871. New ecclesiastical parishes were created, for Southborough in 1831, part of Tunbridge Wells in 1833 and Hildenborough in 1844. Tunbridge Wells was given self government in 1835. The strongest bond of the ancient parish had been the administration of poor relief, which ended in 1834, when the parish was merged with nine others to form a poor law union with a workhouse in Pembury. Until 1871 the Vestry controlled highways, lighting and watching, and drainage for Southborough and Hildenborough as well as the town.

The population of the town rose to 6941 in 1871, more than doubling over 30 years. The opening of the railway from Redhill in 1842 was a principal cause of this rapid growth. Tonbridge became one of the two most important stations in the county, the need for rail staff adding to local employment. The railway strengthened Tonbridge's role as the chief exporting point for the produce of south-west Kent. As Kelly's Kent Directory wrote in 1855, 'the traffic of the town is considerable, by means of the railway and the River Medway'. This helped the town develop further as the major general service centre of the area.

The growth of the town was accompanied by the expansion of its amenities and a surge of house building. A gas company was formed in 1836, a waterworks set up in 1851, and a cattle market built in 1856. The Vestry built brick sewers between 1837 and 1840 which became blocked, many houses being drained by culverts or open ditches connected to the river. Through apathy and the unwillingness of many ratepayers to tax themselves for the benefit of others, the Vestry failed to provide an adequate system of main drainage.

The main area of house building lay in about five new streets lined with dwellings mainly for artisans between the railway and the new wide Pembury Road, running south-east from the Tunbridge Wells road to join the old road to Hastings. They were served by St Stephens, a new church and parish. The importance of building by the 1860s may be shown by the existence in 1866 of so many brickyards on the southern fringes of the town and near the London Road, and four timber yards.

In 1871 new Local Boards of Health were created for Tonbridge and Southborough, giving them powers which they had lacked. Almost immediately the Tonbridge Board provided the much-needed system of main drainage. The opening of the direct rail link to London through Sevenoaks gave a further fillip to growth, though trade on the Medway was on the wane under the competition of the railway.

The Big Bridge photographed from the lower High Street before 1886, showing Blair's printing works (E6), the old Castle Inn (A18) and former Wise's Manufactory (E1). (THS 14A/114)

To house the growing population two new estates were developed at the end of the 1860s and in the 1870s. On Dry Hill three new streets were lined with detached and semi-detached villas built under strict covenants. Nearer the town centre several narrow streets with terraced property were built on the Houselands Estate largely for artisans and unskilled workers. The Public Hall was built in 1874 and two new churches appeared.

Among notable aspects of the society were large numbers working for the railway and in the building trades. 135 men and women had railway jobs in 1871. The builder Edward Punnett, who contracted for the main drainage and the new churches, had 300 building workers and brickmakers in 1871, many of his bricks being presumably exported to London. Another builder, Thomas Dove, employed 72 men. Such figures were of course quite exceptional, with the typical tradesmen or master craftsmen having between one or two and six assistants. The now well-established cricket ball industry had five ball and four bat makers. Another feature was the livestock sales; in the mid-1870s as many as 750-1000 sheep (mostly driven from Romney Marsh) and 100 or 200 cattle were sold at the fortnightly cattle markets before being sent by rail to London. The link with the countryside was still strong and clearly visible.

The Local Board became an Urban District Council in 1894. Their most impressive contribution to the development of the town was the rebuilding of the west side of the High Street south of the Great Bridge between 1892 and about 1912. Between 1891 and 1911 the population rose by nearly a half, from 10,117 to 14,796. The major reason was the advent from London of two printing firms, taking advantage of cheap factory sites and the direct rail link with the capital. Bradbury, Agnew and Co. Ltd. set up in Medway Wharf in a warehouse in 1896 with between 60 and 80 hands. The Dowgate Works of James Truscott and Sons Ltd. bought its Meadow Lawn site for factories to take the entire London staff, numbering between 750 and 850. As

The Big Bridge from the Castle grounds in the 1920s, after the bridge and the buildings on either side had been re-built. Maylam's warehouse is prominent beyond the new Castle Inn. (THS 19/108)

elsewhere in England the growing mass market created by the rising living standards of working families brought multiple stores and cheap bicycles to Tonbridge in the 1890s. For the numerous shopkeepers and professional families there was Frank East's department store and for the wealthy a few motor cars. Middle class education brought a much smaller but still significant impetus to the growth of population. Two girls' private schools and a boys' grammar school began in the 1880s and 1890s. Tonbridge School doubled its boarders in the 1890s, and a girls' secondary school was founded in 1905. While housing appeared in new roads in the north of the town, the largest developments were the Quarry Hill Park Estate in the 1890s and the Meadow Lawn and Blue Barn Estates round the Dowgate Works in the 1900s.

As elsewhere in Britain the normal development of local society in the early 20th century was interrupted by the World Wars in 1914-18 and 1939-45, and the fall in exports by traditional industries in the North, Clydeside and South Wales which caused unemployment even in the south-east. 3000 men (one in five of the population) served in the First World War, with 346 being killed. Both men and women were conscripted in the Second World War, though in both wars women took over men's jobs. Unemployment was rife from 1921 to 1939, reaching a peak early in 1933, when over a thousand men and women were out of work. Population grew slowly from 15,000 in 1911 to about 18,000 in 1946. With all in work enjoying improving living standards shops became more varied and some much bigger, while building and the professions flourished. As wages were still low maids, cleaners, gardeners and street sellers were common. The railway was the greatest single employer, with 650 employees in June 1932. In September 1934 about 700 were working in the various printing factories. The Crystalate Gramophone Manufacturing Company on near the Town Mills had 390 or 400 employees in 1932, cricket ball making still prospered in a small way, and there were little manufactures of goods such as weedkiller and fertiliser. As families were becoming smaller with the fall in the birth rate, council house building flourished in the 1920s and private building in the 1930s. It occurred at the south end of the town and especially in the north and north-east, but not to the east and west where the low-lying meadows were liable to flood. In the 1930s houses had garages or garage sites and petrol stations were being erected. There were two or three cinemas, with 8 or 9 thousand people visiting the Capitol to see 'Snow White' in December 1938. While population rose slowly in the 1950s, from 19,000 in 1951 to 22,000 in 1961, it then grew fast, reaching 30,000 in 1971. Council house building was most important in the decade after the War, then private housing flourished on an unprecedented scale, creating a huge new suburb in the north of the town. Traffic congestion became a problem in the High Street, with local cars, vans and lorries being delayed by longer distance traffic on the main road from Sevenoaks and London to Tunbridge Wells and Hastings. In 1960 the shops on the west of the High Street just north of the Great Bridge were demolished for road widening, while in 1971 an A21 by-pass was opened far outside the town for distance vehicles.

Until the 1970s there was full employment and better living standards for all, with motor cars becoming more and more numerous, and television gradually destroying cinema entertainment. Sports and cultural entertainments continued to flourish, though church going declined. Tonbridge's importance as the centre of education for most of south-west Kent was confirmed with the creation of another girls' grammar school and a secondary technical school. Rail employment fell fast while its use grew with ever more London commuters living in the town. Domestic service disappeared as better education and higher wages drew women into clerical and secretarial employment. The printing works remained, with about 1000 employed in 1960, accompanied with small-scale employment in manufactures such as flints for cigarette lighters, water filters, cooling plants and hot water bottles, tar distilling, egg boxes, pre-cast concrete products, scientific instruments and many other types of goods. Many more shops, the growing professions, administrative offices, laundries, gas, water and electricity undertakings serving the townspeople and the nearby rural inhabitants remained the basic kinds of employment. Finally the Urban District Council ended in 1974 when it was merged into a much larger Tonbridge and Malling District Council, redesignated as a Borough Council in 1983.

A   Agriculture and allied trades

In the earlier sixteenth century, a large part of Tonbridge parish (and modern Tonbridge) was covered by woodland which was part of the Duke of Buckingham's estates. Following his execution for treason against Henry VIII, 5000 acres of woodland in the parish were forfeited in 1553 and eventually leased out, with permission to use all timber for charcoal for the local iron industry for forty years. Before the end of this lease most of the timber from this large area had been used up, and a large part of Tonbridge Manor's demesne land and park land, previously used for deer hunting, had become agricultural land by the second half of the 17th century.

Postern Park Farm in 1965 (THS 3/106)

As in the rest of the low Weald, the land was mainly heavy clay which was difficult to work and had poor natural drainage. As in other parts of the Weald which had been cleared earlier, the Tonbridge farmers in the 17th and 18th centuries tended to have mixed farms with the main income from livestock, especially cattle. Oats (often for feed), wheat and barley (often for brewing) were grown, with small orchards and hopgardens, frequently for the farm's own use.

A pre-1914 postcard by Flemons of Tonbridge showing a typical hop-picking scene of the time. (THS 3/60)

Hop growing became more important in the 19th century, when hopgardens could be seen alongside most of the main roads out of the town. The circular oasts (roundels), in which hops were dried, attached to most farms, mainly date from this period. Higher acreages of hops were linked to the expansion of larger commercial-scale brewing, for example in Tonbridge and Hadlow, which supplied larger areas than the earlier, smaller breweries.

As the main centre of population for the western Weald, Tonbridge town carried much of the infrastructure of agriculture, including warehouses, tannery and fellmonger (A9-A10), corn and hop merchants, breweries (A11-A12), smithies and wheelwrights (D1-D3), timber yards, the cattle market (A22) and mills (B1-B3, B5). Earlier, when the Wealden wool trade was at its height, there were cloth halls (A6-A8) and possibly a fulling mill.

The town was also an important transport centre as market goods, particularly for London, were carried first by road and then by water, when farm carts laden with hops queued to load the barges in Medway Wharf Road. From 1842 the railway greatly eased the transport to market of livestock, fruit and hops from this part of Kent.

From the 1960s, competition and diminishing demand – partly the result of changing drinking habits – brought a rapid decline in fruit and hop-growing, and the annual invasion of West Kent by hop-pickers from London ended in this decade. By this time much of the farmland within the former UDC area had been built over.

Farms and oasts

The swallowing up of land began in the mid-19th century, as the population expanded into new housing built on former farm land, and continued until the late 20th century. In the south of the town, parts of Peach Hall Farm, Priory Farm and Tilehouse Farm were sold off in about 1850. The Dry Hill area in the north, sold in 1865, included two hopgardens, one in the Manor Grove area and the other where Park House now stands in Dry Hill Road. Large areas further north were engulfed during the house-building explosion after World War 2. The large hopgarden

Brook Street Farm (date unknown) – see A2. (THS 3/109)

A   Agriculture and allied trades   25

commemorated by Hopgarden Road, for example, was rooted out in about 1970. Within the boundaries of the former UDC, only a few working farms now survive, mainly in regions adjoining the flood plain. Of more than a dozen farmhouses, mostly with oasts, that once stood within what is now the built-up area of Tonbridge, a number remain, converted to private homes or other use, for example in Brook Street, Bourne Lane and The Ridgeway (A1-A5).

A1   Bourne Farm   ★†
5 Bourne Lane   595472

An oast with two roundels and the adjoining farm house now form a single home, with a former barn alongside, south-east of the grassed area between Haydens and Yardley Park Road. This was a working farm and hopgarden until the 1930s.

A2   Brook Street Farm   ★
Brook Street   580456

This is an L-shaped timber-framed house mostly rebuilt in red brick on the ground floor and tile-hung above. It was the farm house for a dairy farm up to the 1960s. An adjoining barn, shown in the photograph opposite, was destroyed by fire in the 1960s.

A3   Hilden Farm   ★
London Road   581476

The town's most conspicuous surviving oasts are the two roundels of the former Hilden Farm on London Road. Since 1974 they have been part of the Oast Theatre.

A4   Pot Kiln Farm   ●
London Road   584472

Pot Kiln farmhouse stood beside the Hilden Brook, 100 yds to the south of London Road, but has now been demolished. (A pot kiln is an open-topped kiln, but no details of one on this site have been found.) The photograph below shows 'Hand picking at the bin' at one of the farm's hopgardens, c.1960. (THS 3/41)

A5   Cage Farm   ★
77/79 The Ridgeway   594479

The present farm house dates from 1770, and has two parallel ranges and a ground floor in red brick. Other farm buildings stood where the start of Royal West Kent Avenue is now. Until the 1930s a gated track ran up from Hadlow Road along the line of the present Ridgeway. (A gatepost survives at the corner of the lodge, No. 1 The Ridgeway.)

In Henry VIII's time a deer park called The Cage, set with beeches and oaks, occupied the area between the Shipbourne and Hadlow Roads, roughly from The Ridgeway up to Woodland Walk. This became a farm during

†See page 8 for key to symbols.

the reign of Elizabeth I. The land farmed from Cage farmhouse was part of the demesne of the Manor of Tonbridge until it was divided into eight sections after the failure of the male line of the lords of the manor after 1674. Cage Farm, with some 400 acres, was the largest single holding created from the division of the Tonbridge demesne.

Cage Farm was held with Starvecrow Farm, further up Shipbourne Road, from the early 18th century, and in 1838 was more than half arable, nearly a quarter meadow, a fifth woodland, and smaller areas of hops, pasture and orchard. The arable land is likely to have been heavy soil ploughed by large oxen teams. In 1881 the farm was the largest in Tonbridge with 750 acres, and employed 32 men and 7 boys.

When the land held with Cage Farm House was sold for development in the early 1930s it was still a 400-acre holding, and was by then mainly devoted to dairy farming, as were the nearby Cage Green Farm, next to 198 Shipbourne Road, and Dry Hill Farm, behind 15 Shipbourne Road, both of whose farmhouses also survive with cottages alongside.

Tanneries, fellmongery and the cloth trade

Clothmaking flourished in the Weald between about 1350 and 1550, and declined slowly thereafter. Tonbridge, as a meeting point of local roads, was a suitable location for the collection and distribution of textile materials, and three clothiers are known to have been in business in the town in the 16th and 17th centuries. Substantial enterprises such as Cowcheman's (A6) would have relied on dozens of part-time spinners and several weavers, working locally at home. Cowcheman and the other Wealden clothiers sent their finished cloth by wagon to London for sale at Blackwell Hall in Basinghall Street. The processes for changing raw animal hides into durable leather produce foul smells, so tanneries were traditionally sited downwind from centres of population. Both sites in Tonbridge (A9 and A10) were beside streams and on the east side of the town. The process involves soaking the skins in vats of a tannin-rich solution often made from the bark of oak trees, of which there were plenty in the Wealden forests. Tonbridge leather is said to have been of high quality.

A6   Clothier's premises   •
Rear of 39 High Street   589462

Peche Hall was a large house built in the 16th century or earlier to the east of the High Street and 20 or 30 yds south of the present Little Bridge. William Cowcheman, clothier, was the owner and occupier at his death in 1568, when he bequeathed to his eldest son the 'copper, wood fatte, boyling ton and water ton [presumably vats for dyeing] in the workhouse'. Cowcheman also farmed the adjoining 40 acres, and by 1613 the property may have been purely a farm for two or more decades. Much later there was a printing works on the site (see E10).

A7   Clothier's premises   •
River Walk   590464

A clothier's premises lay on the west side of the High Street, south of the Great Bridge and opposite the Castle, in the early 17th century. In 1612 it was occupied by John Cowchman, in 1627 by John Dunck, and in 1648 by David Cheesman, all clothiers; its use before 1612 and after 1648 is not known. Later this was the site of the 19th century brewery (see A11)

A8   Clothier's premises   •
Shipbourne Road/Old London Road   591471

A third clothier's buildings lay on the south side of the junction of Shipbourne Road and the old London Road, just north of the (later) Star and Garter inn, in the mid-17th century. It was leased to Thomas How, clothier, in 1655 and in 1675 by another clothier, John Bannester. How had a copper (large tub) in the workhouse, and a hurdle, 'tainter' (tenter), planks and joists, for stretching the cloth, in his shop .

A   Agriculture and allied trades

A9   Tannery •
Mill Lane   595468

By the seventeenth century Tonbridge had a tannery, with 'tan house, cistern and tannfatts' on its eastern fringe, near the Town Mills and the mill stream. The tannery was held by the Twort family until 1768, and then the Eldridges, who sold out in 1820 to John Waite. The Tithe Map of 1831 shows it as Tan Yard Farm whose 14 acres include a hopgarden (adjacent to what is now Garden Road) and two meadows on the far side of the Mill Stream, now the Golf Range and Swanmead. The 1871 Ordnance Survey map marks the site as Grove House (as it remains today), with the former farmland partly built over.

A separate establishment further down Hadlow Road (600475) is shown as Tanyard Farm. This is a 17th century half timbered building which remains today, with adjoining former cowshed and cottage.

A10   Woolstapler and fellmonger •
Botany   590463

Rowland Stagg was a woolstapler (dealer in wool) and fellmonger (dealer in skins, particularly of sheep) whose works were at Clapper Mead, near the Little Bridge, in the 1870s. The site, which he took over from an earlier fellmonger, is shown on maps of 1866 and 1910 as a tannery, and expanded to fill the rear of Nos. 45 and 47 High Street and the Bull Inn, alongside the Gasworks Stream. A photograph taken in 1890 shows 27 employees. By 1907 the business was using two former square oasts in Bradford Street for wool-drying, and an adjacent warehouse (which later became a cinema – see G10) for storage. These were situated where the Crown Buildings are now.

By the 1920s the Stagg enterprise had expanded onto a site in Botany where it became one of the town's larger industries. Sheds and other buildings here were finally demolished in 1980 when Benn House, now Sovereign House, was built on the site.

The interior of the hide house at Stagg's fellmongery in 1980, just before demolition – see A10. (THS 4/50)

Breweries and inns

For centuries brewing was a domestic activity carried out in the brewhouses of farms, homes and ale-houses. Brewing on a commercial scale was going on in Maidstone, Canterbury and a few other towns in Kent in the 18th century, taking advantage of the ready availability of hops and malt in the county. Tonbridge had its own breweries from early in the 19th century (A11-A12).

There were six inns or public houses in Tonbridge High Street in 1839 (A15-A20), according to Pigot's Directory, and another at Dry Hill (A21). In addition there were two Coaching Inns, the Rose & Crown (A13) and the Bull (A14). More than a dozen stagecoaches called at both these daily, except Sundays, serving London, Brighton, Hastings, Maidstone, St. Leonards, Tenterden and Tunbridge Wells. In later years the number of pubs in the town increased greatly.

A11   Brewery •
River Walk   590464

A brewery and brewer's house were built about 1816 by Anthony Harman of Croydon on the west side of the High Street just south of the main branch of the river, where River Walk now runs. In 1838 the 'house, brewhouse, yard, garden and stable (1 acre 34 perches)'

A view upstream from the Big Bridge, showing the brewery, c. 1818 (A11). Also visible are the public pump (right foreground) and, behind a fence on its right, the horsewash inlet (H21). The print is one of those produced by George Wise (see E1) to decorate the lids of whitewood boxes. (THS 16/30)

were owned and occupied by Harman. By 1866 the 'Bridge Brewery' was owned by William Bartram, who lived there and participated in local affairs. In 1871 he employed 10 men in the brewery, four draymen, a carpenter, bricklayer and four maltsters. Bartram died in 1882, and by 1898 the business was run by a limited company called Bartram, W. and G. Ltd., Brewers and Maltsters. The company was absorbed by the Dartford Brewery Company Ltd., who ran the business until the premises were demolished in road widening, between 1910 and 1913.

A12   Brewery   •

Quarry Hill/Springwell Road   585455

There was a brewery on the east side of the lower part of Quarry Hill by 1839 which lasted at least until 1874, the site being cleared for building in the 1890s (later becoming part of upper St Mary's and Judd Road). In 1839 it was run by William Baker, in 1859 by Benjamin and James Baker and in 1874 by James Taylor Baker.

A13   Coaching Inn   ★

The Rose and Crown, 125 High Street   590466

The Rose and Crown has a typical 18th century brick facade, its interior wooden structure being of 16th century date. Half-timbering is still visible on the rear of the entrance arch. The inn is first mentioned in 1587 as the Crown and a deed of 20 July 1658 refers to it as an 'ancient inn called the Rose and Crowne... [with] ... barns, stables, brewhouse, millhouse, and horse mill'. It became an important coaching inn in the later 18th and early 19th centuries, when its premises also included three adjoining properties in the High Street.

It hosted meetings of local official bodies and voluntary societies in the 18th and 19th centuries, and societies continuing to meet there during the 20th century. During the 19th century elections, candidates addressed the crowd from the portico. Members of the Skinners Company as governors of Tonbridge School stayed there on their annual visitation.

A14   Coaching Inn   •

The Bull, High Street   591468 and 589463

In 1670 the Bull lay on the site of the Terrace, just south of the present Ivy House pub, and had barns, stables, garden and orchard round it; by 1739 it was a 'capital messuage [owner-occupied property] formerly an inn'. By 1835 a Bull Inn lay on the east side of the High Street north of the Little Bridge, in a structure with a painted brick frontage and a timbered interior including a king post. In 1839 it was one of the two principal coaching inns in the town. A supermarket was later built on the site, now occupied by Peacock's store at No. 63 High Street.

The Bull Hotel in the High Street, prior to 1875 — see A14. (THS 14A/110)

A15   Inn   •

The Angel, High Street   588461

The Angel lay an the west side of the High Street, approximately on the site of the entrance to Avebury Avenue, from the 16th to 18th centuries; the earliest references are to the 'messuage or inn called the Angel' or 'le Aungell'. In the 19th century the new Angel, probably built as an inn, lay on the opposite side of the High Street, on the corner of Vale Road. The Angel Hotel was demolished in the early 1970s for a supermarket. Poundstretcher now occupies the site.

A16   Inn   ★

The Chequers, 122 High Street   590465

The Chequers, a 15th century three-storey timbered structure, was an inn by 1739, and is still a public house. According to Neve, it let for £13 in 1790 and £150 in 1820, suggesting a huge jump in property values in the town centre, despite inflation, unless of course there was substantial renovation in the intervening years.

A17   Inn   ★

The Red Lion, 157 High Street   590467

The Red Lion lay on the east side of the High Street just north of Church Lane. Before the 1640s it was known as the George. From 1639 until the early 18th century it was owned by the Weller family of lawyers and local landowners. Leases of the period mention 'wells' and 'boghouses'. It continued under the same name through to 1969. Baldwin's travel agency now occupies the building, 157 High Street.

The Chequers was a popular subject for picture postcards, such as this one from the early 20th century — see A16. (THS 9/32)

A18 Inn ★
The Castle, 89 High Street　　　　　590464

The Castle lies on the east side of the High Street adjoining the south bank of the main River Medway. It was erected as a public house by the Medway Navigation Company in the 1740s, when it was a weather-boarded building. This was demolished for bridge widening in 1886 and the present Castle Inn erected further back on the site.

A19 Inn ●
The Dorset Arms, 34 High Street　　　589462

The Dorset Arms (later Dorset Hotel) on the west side of the High Street near Lambert's Yard was an inn by 1839. A Dorset Arms public house continued at 34 High Street after the road widening until 1961. An Oxfam shop later occupied the site.

A20 Inn ●
The Three Loggerheads, 94 High Street　590464

The Loggerheads is mentioned in the Tonbridge manorial survey of 1739. On the west side of the High Street by the northernmost of the three minor Medway streams, and adjoining the brewery (A11), it remained as a public house and 'Common Lodging House' until demolished for road widening in 1907.

Neve describes it about 1900 as an old inn built of brick and painted a dirty cream colour, with its quaint sign-board: two heads of the bargee or coal-heaver type were painted (not badly) an each side of the sign, and below was the legend 'We three Loggerheads be'. (A Loggerhead is a blockhead; the person looking at the sign was the third.) The Post Office was later built on the site (see G2). It is now the Humphrey Bean pub, named after a proprietor of the Loggerheads in the 1880s.

A21 Inn ★
The George and Dragon, 17 Shipbourne Road　591471

The George and Dragon on the east side of the Shipbourne Road at the top of Dry Hill was an inn by 1839, though its timbered framework with a king post suggests that the building had a sixteenth century origin.

The Market

A weekly general market for produce was probably held in the grounds of Tonbridge parish church prior to 1285 when Edward I banned all fairs and markets in churchyards. The market carried on in what is now the upper High Street, with an overflow on open land to the west, now Bank and Castle Streets, for at least 400 years. A Market Cross stood in the High Street opposite the end of East Street.

　　A Friday general market in the High Street died out in the first half of the 19th century, by which time a Tuesday cattle market was also being held, at first monthly and later more often. The new site for the cattle market in the Slade area (A22) came into use in 1856.

　　Corn Exchanges sprang up around the country in the early 19th century, though Tonbridge did not get its own until 1875 (A23).

　　Hops were of course another important commodity in this area, but the principal trading area was at Southwark in London, where an impressive Hop Exchange building opened in the 1860s (and still survives, at 24 Southwark Street). In Tonbridge, Doust Brothers, Hop and Seed Factors, had premises in the High Street from 1856-90, near where Bradford Street now is – a 'factor' being a dealer who purchases the commodity for himself and then resells it, unlike a broker who mediates deals between others. Another hop factor's nameplate could be seen at the entrance to Central Chambers, 47 High Street, until at least the 1970s.

A   Agriculture and allied trades

A22   Cattle Market   •
Bank Street/The Slade   589467

Tonbridge Stock and Cattle Market Company was formed in 1855 and set up a new market place on open land in the Slade area which came into use the following year. Pens and other market buildings were set up. Stock for sale was brought from a wide area. In the early years many animals were transported by rail, unloading at a special platform adjacent to Vale Road, and being driven up the High Street, but lorry transport later became the norm.

The stock market flourished into the 20th century with as many as 500 pigs, 2-300 sheep and 100 cattle changing hands on occasion, and more than 50 prospective buyers in attendance. In the year to August 1955, 46,000 animals were auctioned, including cows, calves, bulls, sheep, goats, pigs and poultry. Operations finally ceased in 1971 following an outbreak of foot and mouth disease.

The Stock and Cattle Market Company retained the site, which was used for a Saturday general market until 2003, when it was sold for residential and commercial development. See also H16.

A23   Corn Exchange   ★
Bank Street   590467

A handsome Meeting-House or Chapel was completed in Back Lane, now Bank Street, for protestant dissenters in 1791. In 1875, after the dissenters, who eventually became the United Reform Church, moved to a new church at the south end of the High Street, the Meeting-House was purchased by the Tonbridge Stock and Market Company for use as a Corn Exchange. (Before then, corn had been bought and sold on the basis of samples brought by farmers to a market held in the Angel Inn on Monday evenings.) The building has recently been in use as offices.

B   Water and wind power

The River Medway, and particularly its local tributary sometimes known as the Bourne or Somerhill Stream, have provided power for several mills or other works in and close to the Tonbridge urban area. Six sites where this form of power was certainly used are shown on the map on page 13. A further three sites where some uncertainty exists at present are also shown. At none of these places are there now substantial remains of the industry and no waterwheels are thought to exist, but at Town Mills a small, long disused, turbine is still in place. Although the rivers have a rather low gradient, by means of mill dams and suitable leats (man-made channels) sufficient head could be obtained for the use of mainly breast-shot wheels. Industries using water power included corn milling, gunpowder manufacture and iron smelting and forging. It is possible that an early fulling mill also existed locally.

The use of water-power for grinding corn and for other purposes was probably introduced to Britain by the Romans and at a small number of sites remains of mills have been excavated. By the time of the Domesday survey over five thousand mills are recorded, but Tonbridge is not referred to directly in that document. It seems highly likely, however, that a manorial mill would have been present at this relatively important centre. Allowing that watermill sites, once established, are very rarely moved, it is reasonable to suppose that this mill would have been at the location of the Town Mills (B1). The earliest documentary reference to a mill at Tonbridge is in Memoranda Rolls dated 1326-7 but again it is impossible to be sure of location. There is a passing mention of 'Bournemelne' (Bourne Mill) in 1340 (see B7). Further references to mills occur, sparsely, through the 16th and 17th centuries but not until the mid-18th century can documents be linked accurately to existing sites.

Two other corn mills have operated in or near Tonbridge, at Ramhurst on the Leigh boundary (B5), and the Priory Mill south of the town (B2). The former mill closed down and was demolished when the important gunpowder mills were developed nearby in the early 19th century.

Water-power played an important part in the long-extinct 'Wealden' iron industry. The High Weald area became the most important iron-producing region of Britain from Roman times onwards, reaching its peak of production in Tudor times. Tonbridge lies at the northern margin of the main producing area but nevertheless research has located up to five sites where water-power was used within the parish of Tonbridge. A brief note about iron ore extraction is included in section C (Extractive Industry) on page 38. In the early, so-called 'Bloomery' period of the industry iron was produced by the direct process, ore being smelted in simple kiln-like furnaces, with bellows perhaps operated by water-power. After the introduction of the blast-furnace in the late 15th century water-power became widely used, not only to drive larger bellows at furnace sites but also to power hammers at the numerous forges.

B Water and wind power

All the ironworks locally were situated on the Somerhill (Bourne) Stream and they include two furnace sites and two forges, one of which (Rat's Castle) is now considered to have been a water-powered medieval bloomery. More details of these sites are given in the gazetteer (B6-B9). A problematic site at present is Bourne Mill Farm, south of the town and close to the A21 main road. Referred to on old maps as simply Bourn Mill, it was surely a water-powered site but so far no trace of a watermill has been found. It is possible that the name comes from the nearby Bournemill furnace, or was this the actual site of the furnace?

Wind-power has been much less important in our area. Much is known about a mill in the Cage Green locality, working during the 19th century (B10) and there is some evidence of two others: a document of 1775 describes the Town Mill in Mill Lane as standing on the 'site of a windmill recently burnt down', while the 1838 Tithe map shows a 'windmill field' on Quarry Hill.

B1 Corn Mill: Town Mills ★

Town Mills, Mill Lane   595467

This water-powered corn mill is presumably the one on record as operating in Tonbridge in 1326, and probably existed for some centuries before then. Today only the 17th century mill cottage remains, with brick-paved hardstanding in front, and low buildings alongside which house the remains of an early 20th-C iron water-turbine. The Mill Stream which in earlier years carried all the water from the branch of the Medway that flows past the Castle, flows through into a downstream pool from which the stream continues.

William Mercer was miller in 1787, but became bankrupt in 1800 at which time there were two mills under one roof. William and John Jewhurst owned the mill in 1819 and added a new mill, with large warehouse adjoining, across the road from the old one, before selling it for the huge sum of £20,000 to James Christie in 1829 (see page 87).

From the 1830s to 1897 the mill was in the hands of John Sills Charlton, farmer, miller and member of the Local Board. By 1871 a steam-powered mill, with tall chimney, had been added as a result of which less water was flowing through the mills causing the mill-pond to fill up and become a cesspool. When the next owner, H. J. Symonds and Co., sold the mill in 1907 it comprised the 'New Flour Mill having four floors and offices, and the Old Mill with 3 floors, mill house, mill stream and all

The old Town Mill, perhaps c.1900. The present Mill Cottage is at the far end, while the water wheels were beneath the central portion. (THS 5/85)

water rights'. The water power was said to be 'enormous and continuous'. A report dated 1941 described the Old Mill as having had two iron breast-shot wheels driving two pairs of stones, while the New Mill had a large breast wheel driving four pairs of stones. The Steam Mill had been powered by a horizontal steam engine but also had a small Poncelet (undershot) waterwheel to drive a hoist. All trace of these mills had gone.

The corn mill is said to have continued operating until the First World War. The site was purchased by the Urban District Council in 1918 in order to obtain control over the water flow. Storey Motors (see E13) installed their own turbines and there may have been as many as five wheels or turbines in operation on occasions, taking so much water that the level was lowered all the way up the river and navigation prevented.

Electricity generation continued at the New Mill until at least 1938, and other concerns then occupied some of the buildings until 1970 when they were demolished for road-widening.

Parts of a turbine used to convert water power to electricity remain under the Town Mill. It bears the name 'Stilwell and Bierce Manufacturing Co., Dayton, Ohio' and probably dates from the first quarter of the 20th century. The photograph below shows the turbine casing as it was in 2002. In use, water entered near the top and turned the wheel, whose axis is vertical, as it descended. An overhead drive (not visible) linked the turbine to an electrical generator alongside.

B2 Corn Mill: Priory Mill ☆

Five Oak Green Road 601455

Priory Mill was opened in the early 19th century and has no connection with the medieval priory in the town. It stands on land which is now part of the Wallace and Tiernan site (see E17) and was served by a leat, now filled in, from the Bourne stream near Somerhill. A mill is shown on Mudge's map of Kent (early 19th century) though not on the 1838 Tithe Map. From c.1840 William Cushion owned the mill, and from 1870 until 1921 it was in the hands of the Seabrook family. The Charlton brothers took it over and also grew hops at the adjacent Priory Mill Farm. Fire destroyed the mill in 1938, but a survey in 1947 found the building repaired, and the waterwheel still inside, overshot, about 6 feet in diameter and 2.5 ft wide, together with 6 pairs of millstones on two floors above.

In 2001 there was no trace of the wheel or other mechanism, though the building remained, along with the miller's house, which was under threat of demolition, and the farm buildings with two oasts.

B3 Water Mill: Bourne Mill ☆

South-east of Vauxhall Lane 597445

The name and situation beside the Somerhill Stream, and early map designations simply as Bourne Mill or Burn Mill leave no doubt this was a water-powered site, but the location of a millwheel cannot now be determined. There is evidence of a mill here by 1340, and it has been suggested this was the site of an early fulling mill (where woollen cloth was beaten to increase its weight and thickness), and also the site of 'an iron furnace worked by the iron master John Kipping'. From at least the 17th century the site has been known as Bourne Mill Farm. The local topography suggests perhaps a mill pond behind a dam to the south-east of the farm on a minor tributary to the Somerhill Stream. The present complex includes farmhouse, cottages and farm buildings all known as Bourne Mill Farm. See also site B7.

B4 Gunpowder Mills: Leigh ☆

Powdermill Lane 597466

Gunpowder manufacture began on a 14-acre site at Ramhurst in Leigh in 1813, when demand was high during the Napoleonic wars.

B Water and wind power

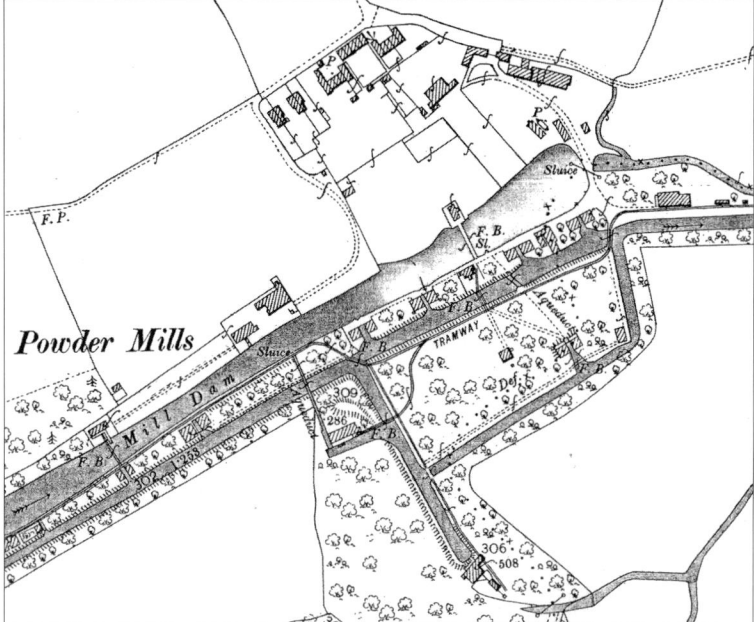

The Powder Mills site in 1897

The venture was set up by George Children of Ferox Hall, James Burton of Mabledon, and others, including for a short while the scientist Sir Humphry Davy, initially to manufacture powder for sporting use.

The process required water-power for grinding the ingredients to a very fine powder and for the 'incorporating' mills which mixed the powders in the form of a paste. A long leat from and parallel to a branch of the Medway (labelled Mill Dam on the map above) provided power for the waterwheels, several of which were sited between this dam and the parallel channel below it which took the tail water. The waterwheels were breast-shot, with a 10-foot) head of water. Waterways were also used for transporting materials around the site by barge and for carrying the finished product out to the Medway.

From 1824 to 1859 the works was in the hands of the Burton family, the original partnership having been dissolved. The works was sold to C. B. and T. Curtis (later Curtis and Harvey) in 1859, who owned other powder mills in the region. At that time the Leigh premises included a charcoal kiln, grinding and mixing houses, a petre refinery and mill, and four further mills driving 8 pairs of stones. There was also a 12-room manager's house overlooking the site, 15 cottages for workmen (see photo B4a), and a Thames-side storage magazine at Erith. Output was said to be 7,000 to 14,000 barrels of gunpowder a year (300 to 600 tons), and profits £2-3000 a year. The factory was then mainly producing powders for military use, but by 1909 the army was using cordite instead of powder, and production shifted to smokeless sporting powder, in addition to other explosives.

An explosion in 1916 caused chunks of metal to fall on Tonbridge, but production carried on until 1934. Chemical manufacture and research continued on an adjacent site which is today part of the GlaxoSmithKline (GSK) pharmaceuticals conglomerate. The area covered by the original powdermills (owned by GSK) is Tonbridge's prime industrial archaeology site, and awaits a full investigation. Structures such as wheelpits (see photo B4b overleaf), foundations and millstones (photo B4c) remain, as do the manager's house and workers' cottages.

B4a

Photo: F. Tullett

Photo: F. Tullett

Photo: F. Tullett

B5 Corn Mill: Ramhurst Mill •

River Medway, Ramhurst, nr. Leigh   566464 approx.

A large corn mill formerly stood at the southern end of the lane opposite the drive to Ramhurst Manor, at the western end of the later Powdermills site. It size is indicated by the statement that 'it could be driven by the whole flow of the Medway' and it may have employed several millers, serving a larger area than the nearby parish. The sunken lane on its approach may be the result of the large amount of traffic. In 1579 the heirs of Michael Weston owned the mill. It then passed through various other hands until 1626 after which it was leased or owned by the Webb family for the next 120 years. Ramhurst Mill was demolished in c.1812 to allow the widening of the millstream during construction of the powdermills.

B6 Ironmaking furnace: Vauxhall ★

Vauxhall Lane near Moat Farm   592440

Remains of the pond bay (dam) that held back water for the Vauxhall furnace are marked on the latest 1:25000 Ordnance Survey map, and much slag (stony byproduct of the blast furnace process) has been found nearby. The furnace was in action by 1552 when it was owned by the Duke of Northumberland, Lord of the Manor. It was later operated by a sub-tenant, Davy Willard, who also built the Postern Forge (see B8). Iron ore would have been extracted locally, perhaps in Minepit Wood, 593424, or in another wood of the same name at 582431. Ponds, some now dry, alongside Vauxhall Lane near the Cottage Hospital may also be remnants of the iron industry. Iron from the furnace would have been taken to the associated forge, a kilometre upstream at what is now Brokes Mill Farm, 593428.

B7 Ironmaking furnace: Bourne Mill •

Bourne Stream, about 0.5 m N. of B6   ?594443

Surviving accounts concerning Tudeley ironworks mention another ironworks at 'Newefrith juxta Bournemelne' in 1340, owned by Elizabeth de Burgh, the 'Lady of Clare'. Chalklin has recently presented evidence for a furnace downstream from Vauxhall furnace. Davy Willard was also tenant here in 1564, but by 1615 it was inactive, being known as 'the Old Furnace'. Its location has not yet been confirmed by evidence on the ground, and the relation between this site and the Bourne Mill Farm site (B3) is unclear at present.

B8 Ironmaking forge: Postern ★

Postern Lane   605462

Postern Lane itself runs along what may have been the bay that held back water for this forge, though the pond no longer remains. The forge was set up by Davy Willard in the 1550s. Postern Forge House, 606462, is believed to be contemporary with it, and evidence in the form of cinder, parts of the forge, and cannon balls have been found there.

B   Water and wind power

B9   Bloomery: Rat's Castle ●
NE. of the Postern   612466

A quantity of forge cinder has been found at this site, which is reached down a track from The Postern. It was thought at one time to have been a forge site, but more recent research suggests there was a medieval bloomery here.

B10   Windmill: Cage Green ●
36 Uridge Road   590475

Brothers Edgar and Isaac Uridge owned Cage Green Windmill in the 1830s (and also operated a windmill in Southborough). The Tonbridge mill stood at the west end of what is now Uridge Road (No. 36). It had a brick base with an upper part that could be rotated to face the wind by a horse harnessed to a wooden beam. Edgar Uridge was also a corn dealer and there is said to have been a bakery nearby. A lane led to the mill from Spring Hill, now Shipbourne Road, and part of this remains, skirting the south side of the Shell Filling Station. Isaac Uridge died in 1844 and his brother in 1853, after which the mill passed through various hands before falling out of use by the late 1860s. It was demolished in about 1872 when the area was built over.

Uridge's windmill (B10) can be seen in the background on the right of this photograph. The gated track, known as The Slype, is now Yardley Park Road. (THS 15/YPR/1)

C   Extractive industry

From very early times the varied rocks of the Tonbridge area have yielded useful materials for constructional and other purposes, but, with the exception of gravel working at the Postern, extractive industry no longer takes place in the district. However, at certain periods this kind of economic activity seems to have been quite important and indeed, one of the principal thoroughfares of the town is called Quarry Hill Road. The quarry or quarries referred to are uncertain and have now probably disappeared.

The geological background to the town has been outlined in an earlier section (pages 13-16), and is shown in simplified form in the map on page 15. Quarrying for stone and sand (C1-C9) took place mainly on the higher ground south of the town where these materials could be extracted from the Hastings Beds formation. Brick and tile works (C10-C22) were widely distributed, making use of clays from the same strata but also from the Weald Clay formation towards the north. So-called 'Brickearth' deposits were used in some places. Commercial gravel winning (C23-C28) has been confined to the alluvial deposits of the Medway valley, while the name Loampits Close, off Hadlow Road (599472) suggests yet another quarrying activity of former times. Loam was dug either for agricultural use or for use in brickmaking.

Another former quarrying or perhaps 'mining' activity in our area which should be mentioned briefly was the extraction of suitable ore, usually a clay-ironstone, for the Wealden iron industry. This was obtained mainly from the Wadhurst clay, a division of the Hastings Beds. Several smelting sites or bloomeries have been tentatively identified in the extensive woodlands south of the town, a remnant of the great South Frith chase. One of these is the well documented Tudeley ironworks whose exact location is unclear. For these works and for the later water-powered furnaces (see section B, pages 36-37) ore was obtained from shallow workings sometimes, inaccurately, known as bell-pits from their supposed shape. Remains of these, often now water-filled, can be found in several localities, one of which is the appropriately named Minepit Wood (593434). It should be noted that 'mine' is an old name for the ore.

Stone Quarrying

Most of the rocks outcropping in the area have at one time or another been exploited and at least from early mediaeval times stone quarrying has been carried out. Numerous small quarries worked the sands and sandstones, no doubt for purely local use in farm buildings, creation of paths and trackways and so on. The sandstones are in the main rather friable and therefore unsuitable as true building stone but at some locations a well-cemented stone does occur and this has provided a lasting material for some of the older buildings in Tonbridge, most notably the castle, the parish

C Extractive industry

church and some of the prominent houses such as Somerhill and Mabledon. A division of the Hastings Beds known as Ardingly Sandstone is found close to our area and this massive, hard sandstone may well have supplied the stone for building the castle. A source at Barden Park, or perhaps higher up the Medway near Leigh has been suggested, though suitable stone could also have been brought down from Quarry Hill, a much closer provenance. In later centuries, following the dereliction of the castle, its stonework was removed in large quantities, and numerous walls and building plinths can still be seen which probably made use of this recycled material.

It has been reported that the mansion Mabledon was possibly built of stone quarried on site in about 1800. The south aisle of Tonbridge Church, constructed in 1877, is also said to be of local stone, and in recent times restoration work at Somerhill made use of stone from the estate's own quarry. This quarry is yet to be located.

The geological map on page 15 shows the location of the more significant quarries recorded on early Ordnance Survey maps and/or noted by the Geological Survey when this area was surveyed in the 1930s. Most of these excavations would have been for useful stone or sand but at site C8 clay was dug, possibly for use at the Vauxhall brickyard (C13). Brief gazetteer entries are given for these quarries but all workings are long disused, overgrown, and in some cases no longer exist. Chapman mentions an additional quarry in Shipbourne Road. This may have been on the site now filled with town houses at the north end of Dernier Road.

Stonework in the castle, possible quarried at Barden Park (see C1).

Recycled stone from the castle in the wall of No. 212 High Street, in Lansdowne Road.

Photos: F. Tullett

C1 Old Quarry ★
Barden Park   579466

Massive sandstone was quarried here and a face up to 10 ft high still remains behind the recent bungalow development. This is penetrated by two shallow chambers, now bricked up, the purpose of which is uncertain. Barden Park area is a possible source of the stone for Tonbridge Castle.

C2 Old Pits –
North bank of R. Medway, East of Leigh   556462

Ardingly sandstone was quarried here. It is another source suggested for the stone for Tonbridge Castle.

C3 Roadside Pits ●
Upper Hayesden   565448

Thin sandstones and a shelly limestone were formerly quarried here from the Wadhurst Clay formation. No trace remains.

C4 Old pits –
Upper Hayesden   565445

A sandrock was formerly quarried here from the Ashdown Beds formation.

C5 Old Pit –
N. of Nightingale Farm, to E. of A26   582443
A bluish-grey limestone was dug here from the Wadhurst Clay formation.

C6 Old quarry ☆
Just west of Forest Farm, in Quarry Wood   595439
This quarry yielded mainly fine grained sandstone and sandy clays.

C7 Old pit –
Mabledon Farm, E. of A26   589445
Massive sandstone was quarried here. This is a possible source of stone for Mabledon House.

C8 Old Pit ●
Priory Wood, 450 yds W. of the Vauxhall Inn   591450
Clays and ironstones of the Wadhurst Clay formation were once worked here. The site was just possibly the source of material for the Vauxhall Brickyard (C13), but has been obliterated by later works.

C9 Old roadside quarry ●
Postern Lane, 150 yards S-E. of The Postern   608461
Massive sandstone was formerly quarried here, but no indication can be seen today.

Brick and Tile making

These have been much more important than stone-quarrying in the more recent history of the town, and intimately connected with its expansion in the 19th century and since. Again, none of this activity remains, but the locally important Quarry Hill brickworks closed only in the 1990s. All known sites of brickmaking are also shown on the map on page 15. The distribution gives some indication of the importance of Brickearth deposits and the Weald Clay for the supply of raw materials. The earliest positively identified sites date from the early 19th century but documentary evidence points to brickmakers living in Tonbridge as early as the mid-17th century.

Fine brick houses in the town, such as Ferox Hall and Old Judd House (part of Tonbridge School) and numerous High Street brick facades are of Georgian date, but the provenance of the bricks used is as yet uncertain. Production of bricks and tiles locally seems very likely to have commenced or at least received a large boost, following the canalisation of the River Medway in the 1740s. Clearly, this made it much easier to bring bulky raw materials to the town, including chalk for making lime, an essential ingredient of mortar and not readily obtainable hereabouts. A large brickmaking industry had now developed on the lower Medway so it is possible that bricks for the earlier town houses were imported from North Kent. By the early 19th century brick had certainly become the common building material here, replacing the centuries-old tradition of timber-framed construction. Nearly all the older streets of the town contain houses built with locally produced bricks and in some cases the building firms were also the brick manufacturers.

Adjoining sections of wall outside The Priory in Bordyke are built of standard bricks (left) and outsize ones – probably used to avoid paying the Brick Tax which was levied between 1784 and 1850.

About a dozen brickmaking sites have been identified within or very close to the

C Extractive industry

Products of the Quarry Hill brickworks – see C11).

town area, using all editions of the Ordnance Survey maps and one or two earlier sources. Nomenclature varies for the sites, from 'brickfield' or 'brickyard' to 'brickworks' and 'brick and tile works'. Hand-made brick production involved the extraction of clay from shallow pits, its moulding to shape in wooden moulds, drying the bricks in rows under the cover of 'hacks', and firing either in clamps or in specially constructed kilns. In earlier times bricks were often made at or close to the site where they would be used, and workers were frequently itinerant. Later, more substantial works were developed, producing a range of products. Some early maps give a good idea of the layout of the plants, e.g. C15, C16 and C20.

At only a couple of sites have physical remains of the industry been discovered, and these are described in the gazetteer. Other sites are recalled simply in local names such as Brickworks Close and Brickyard Cottages.

A 'pottery' existed in the 19th century in Shipbourne Road, but the source of its raw material or indeed information about its products is not yet established.

C10 Brickfield ●

Woodfield Road area 588455-590456

A brickfield of 3 acres in this area, occupied by George Punnett, is listed in the Tithe Apportionment Roll of 1838 (Plot No. 1714) but no detail is shown in the accompanying map. By the late 1850s a considerable brickworks is shown on the O.S. First Edition maps, clearly with kilns and drying-sheds. This must be the site where Punnetts commenced their operations and thereafter became a prominent name in local brickmaking and construction. A record of 1858 mentions the 'manufacture of bricks, tiles and drainpipes – 2,000,000 per annum', and by 1870-1 it seems that 300 men were employed here in brickmaking and a large woodyard. Raw materials may have come from the adjacent Priory Farm where Marlpit Field (Plot 1720 on the Tithe Map) was jointly owned by Punnett, but also possibly from a quarry further up the hill to the south, clearly shown on the First Edition maps. This quarry later became the site of brickworks C11. Site C10 is not shown on maps of 1898, and by 1907 the area was completely residential. The area around the junction of Woodfield and Springwell Roads is the former brickworks site.

Punnett was also a builder, appearing in the 1851 census as 'Master builder', with 15 employees, and in an 1859 Directory as 'builder, stonemason, statuary, stone and slate merchant' in addition to brick and tile maker and farmer. The firm was responsible for several important buildings in the town, including St Stephen's Church, opened in 1852, Tonbridge School's main building in 1864, and the enlargement of Mabledon in 1870. They were also extensively involved in housing development in the quadrant between Quarry Hill and Pembury Road. By 1871 George's son Edward was in charge of 'Punnett and Sons'. Under his leadership, the firm improved the town's drainage, restored the Parish Church, and built a new Science Block for Tonbridge School. By 1932 the building business was based at 220 Vale Road, and it was still operating from there in the 1970s. The premises remain (597459), though currently unoccupied. Memorials to George Punnett and several of his descendants are in St. Stephen's churchyard, in a plot adjoining the south wall of the church he built.

C11 Quarry Hill brickworks •

N. of Baltic Road, near Quarry Hill   587449

This works, established by Punnetts by 1898, became the most important brickworks in Tonbridge and the longest lasting, finally closing only in the 1990s. It seems most likely that the family moved operation up to this site in the 1890s, preparatory to developing the area around their other brickworks (C10) for housing. Throughout its life the upper site was known as the Quarry Hill Brickworks but was operated by a succession of owners following the Punnetts, including the Sussex Brick Co., The Sussex and Dorking United Brick Co. Ltd., and finally becoming part of the Redland Group in the late 1950s.

Clay, and also sand, were obtained from the adjacent quarry, shown on the map and in the photograph below. This appears on the 1860 O.S. map so may previously have supplied the C10 brickworks. By 1923 the Quarry Hill works was capable of producing 100,000 bricks a week, according to a notice of sale which describes it as 'exceptionally well planned and equipped', with 'very complete modern machinery...'. Output in 1955 was 80,000 bricks a week, including some hand-made ones, from a workforce of 40 men, and similar figures applied in the mid 1980s. At that time output was equally divided between machine-made and hand-made bricks. The latter were a speciality, with the brickworks employing the largest number of hand brickmakers at any one site in the country – 12

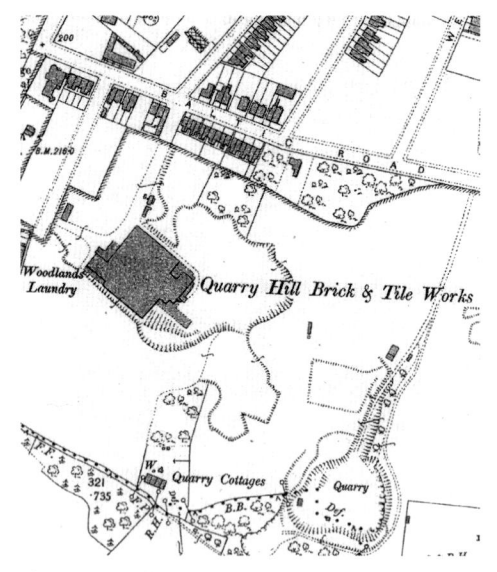

The Quarry Hill brickworks site in 1909.

Tonbridge Brickworks and quarry in 1966. (THS 4/94)

C   Extractive industry

men, each producing 4-5000 bricks a week. These were made in specialised colours, textures and sizes, and used in restoration work, for example at Hampton Court Palace and Chevening House.

After production ceased the tall brickworks chimney was demolished by Fred Dibnah in 1993. Brickworks Close, Hilltop, and adjacent roads now occupy the site.

A 'Tonbridge' range of hand-made bricks, made elsewhere, is still available from Ibstock Brick, which took over the Redland brick business in 1996.

C12   Brickfield   ●

Priory Road area   593458

No brickworks existed here at the date of the Tithe Map, 1838, the land being part of Relf's Farm with meadow, woodland and arable area. By the 1860s, First Edition O.S. maps, a substantial works is shown in some detail, with hacks (covered drying sheds) and kilns in a site totally enclosed by a triangle of railway tracks. Operations continued until the 1880s but soon after this the works must have closed, because the Second Edition O.S. maps of 1898 show housing covering the site – Rose Street and Pembury Grove.

Nothing is yet known of the operator of this brickfield and there is no map evidence of excavation of raw materials. It is possible that clay and sand from the adjacent railway cuttings and tunnel was used.

C13   Vauxhall Brickyard   ●

Pembury Road, just W. of the Vauxhall Inn   595451

This was probably the first brickworks operated by the Chalklin family, dating from the first decades of the 19th century. The Tithe Map of 1838 shows structures which may be drying-sheds and the Apportionment Roll describes the site (Plot No. 1832) as 'rough and meadow' but with 'Brickfield Cottage and Garden' and the occupier as William Chalklin. It appears that the works closed in the 1840s and was superseded by a larger concern at Lavender Hill (C14)

C14   Brickfield/brickworks   ●

E. of Lavender Hill, next to railway   592455

This site was acquired by William Chalklin in the 1840s or 50s and became an important local brickworks for many years. It remained in the family until production ceased, probably at about the time of World War 1. A report to the Council suggested that in 1918 it could be operated to produce bricks for houses then much needed in the town. Drayton Road now occupies part of the brickworks site.

Early O.S. maps show detailed layout with hacks and possibly a kiln. No clay pit is adjacent but the works is next to the long spoil heap from construction of the nearby railway tunnel and perhaps that material was used. A report of 1858 talks of 'marly clay' being worked, and a production of 300,000 bricks per annum. William Chalklin was also a builder, responsible for many of the houses on the south side of Pembury Road.

C15   Brickfield/brickworks   ★

Castle Hill, S. side of A21   605444

In the 1838 Tithe Apportionment Roll this site is described as Castle Hill Brickyard and is occupied by a Mr Mellor. Forming part of the Somerhill Estate, it comprised a brickyard, pits, shaws, and mills (presumably animal-

Part of a billhead from Vauxhall Brickyard (C13) (THS Archives)

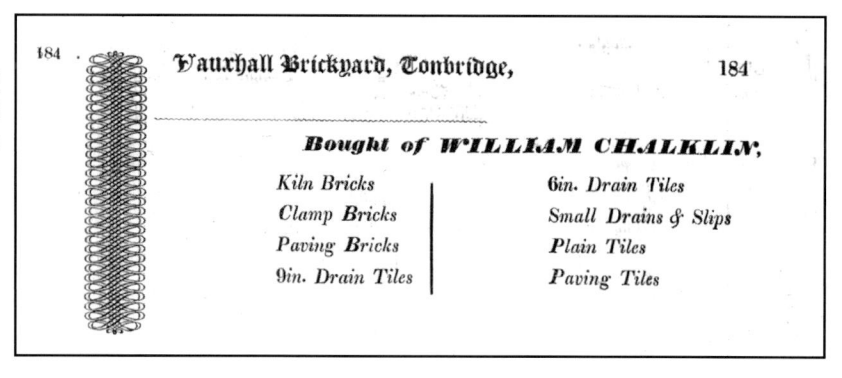

Vauxhall Brickyard, Tonbridge,

Bought of WILLIAM CHALKLIN,

Kiln Bricks   6in. Drain Tiles
Clamp Bricks   Small Drains & Slips
Paving Bricks   Plain Tiles
9in. Drain Tiles   Paving Tiles

powered pug mills) as well as a woodyard. The accompanying map, unlabelled, shows various buildings including what must surely be drying-sheds or hacks.

It seems to have been a typical rural works, producing hand-made bricks and tiles in wood-fired kilns and probably operating only part-time. A photograph dated 1889 indicates that there were about 16 employees including 3 youths, the owner then being Mr Edward Wheatley. Operations ceased some time in the 1920s, the last kiln being demolished in the 1930s when the site became a piggery.

Almost all traces of the works have now been obliterated either by roadworks or landfill. In a very overgrown area, very near to the A21 and close to the original site, there remains a small brick-dammed pond which has existed for over a century. It may or may not be connected with the old brickworks.

C16   Brickworks ☆
E. of Lower Haysden Lane, 0.5m SW. of Haysden   565453

Little has been found about the brickworks that operated on this site in the early 20th century. It is listed as Hayesden Brick Co. in Kelly's directories between 1907 and 1911. The layout is shown on the 1909 O.S. map (see below), including small pits, one of which is connected to the kiln by what may be a conveyor.

A house ('Chartfield') now occupies the site, beneath which, reached by a trapdoor, is an underground chamber some 8 feet high and 8 feet in diameter. This is probably a 'blunger pit' in which clay was rendered very fluid so that stones and pebbles could be worked out, prior to the clay being used for tilemaking.

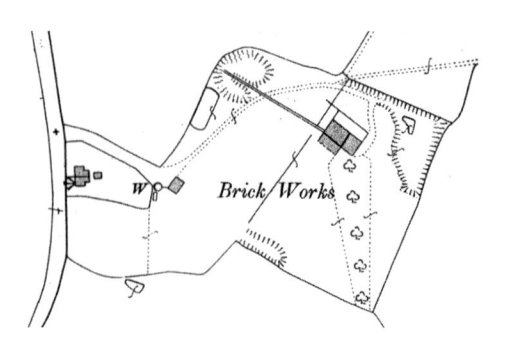

Haysden brickworks (C16), in 1909. Lower Hayesden Lane is on the left.

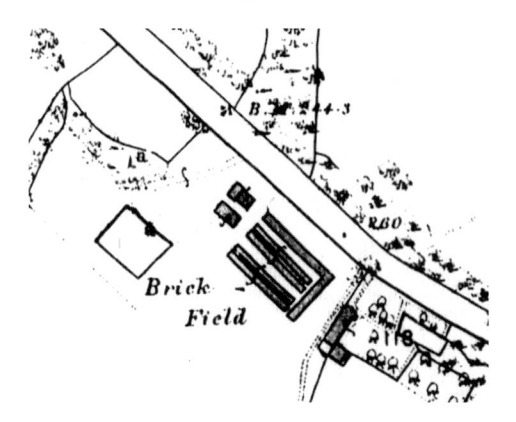

Castle Hill brickworks (C15), c.1870. The Hastings Road (now A21) runs alongside.

C17   Brickworks ●
London Road   584473

A brickworks is shown on the west side of Hilden Brook, south-west of Hilden Bridge, in the 1860s but had gone by 1897, and nothing can now be found. It was owned in the 1870s by Dennis Charlton. The brickworks was just across the stream from Pot Kiln Farm, also now demolished, whose name presumably records an earlier use of the brickearth found at this location.

C18   Brickyard ●
E. side of Shipbourne Road, Dernier Rd area   592477

The 1838 Tithe Map shows cottages and a brickyard alongside Shipbourne Road, with 4 or 5 hacks and a pond, the occupier being Henry Barrett. Directories of 1847 and 48 list Henry Larkin as brickmaker at Cage Green, but the yard is not shown on the 1860s O.S. map, and nothing can now be seen.

C19   Brickworks ★
W. side of Shipbourne Road   594488

This was a small works with apparently a very short life, operating from about 1934 until 1939. Hand-made bricks were produced, being fired in clamps and breeze-blocks were also manufactured. The bricks were reportedly still being sold during World War 2.

The clay-pit and plant lay in the area behind the former St. Bernard's Garage, north of the present York Parade. Two cottages beside the main road, known as Brickyard Cottages, which presumably housed some of the

C Extractive industry

workers, are extant – see photo below. The works was owned and operated by W. C. Chalklin.

C20 Brickworks ☆
Shipbourne Road, opp. Aldwych Guards Close   598 495

The 1838 Tithe Map indicates a claypit at this location, which lies just over the former Tonbridge boundary in Hadlow parish. Census data from 1851 show a brickmaker here, Joseph Mann, and two drainpipe makers (his sons), and the site was still active in 1907, according to the O.S. map of that year, which marks 'Starvecrow Brickworks', with kiln, 4 hacks and claypit. Production appears to have ceased by 1936. Two houses occupy the site today, together with two hacks now serving as outbuildings – the only brickmaking hacks known to survive in the area. The site is private.

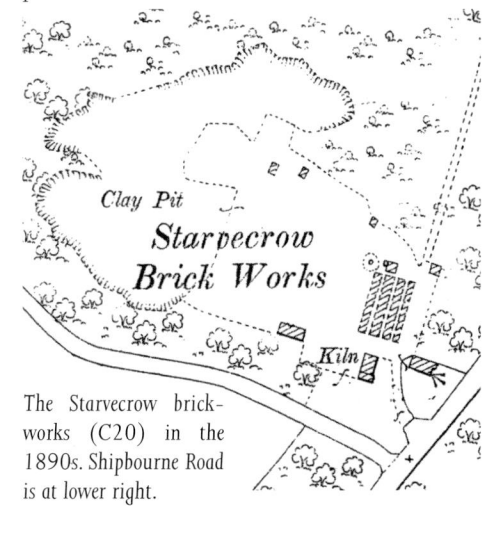

The Starvecrow brickworks (C20) in the 1890s. Shipbourne Road is at lower right.

C21, C22 Brick and Tile Works ☆
Pittswood   615494   Poult House   613497

Both sites are south of Ashes Lane, in the Pittswood area, just beyond the Tonbridge boundary. They are close together and it has not been possible to disentangle records regarding ownership or production. A pottery is shown hereabouts on a map of 1801, and by 1842 (Tithe Map) a brickyard is clearly shown at site C21. Other features on the map which indicate probably activity to the north include Great and Little Kiln Fields, Claypit Field and Poult House Pit. Not until the 1890s (2nd edition O.S.) is a separate works shown at site C22 but by then the Pittswood concern is unlabelled and possibly closed. It seems likely that the two works were run by the same operator, and in the early 20th century (1909 O.S.) site C21 is apparently active once more while the Poult House works is clearly closed. A final closure date is uncertain at present.

From 1840 the owner/operator was George Richardson of Poult House who combined brickmaking with farming. His son, also George, is described in 1871 as a 'brownware manufacturer'. By the 1890s the business had passed to the Palmer family who were also only part-time brickmakers.

Today a curious 'Gothick' house stands on the Pittswood site, set down within an attractive landscaped depression which could once have been a quarry. Round-headed openings in the basement or podium of the new house are quite kiln-like. A number of shallow basins in the wood nearby can be seen from a public footpath and are likely to be former claypits. Hornbeam trees from this wood are said to have been used for fuel. North-east of Poult House a long linear depression is undoubtedly the site of clay-winning for the brickworks here – see photograph below.

Gravel extraction

The only extractive industry to make an important impact locally in recent years is the winning of gravel. Alluvial deposits along the Medway valley have proved to be of considerable value and quarrying has proceeded at several sites with workings being opened successively downstream. Evidence for former extraction is mainly in the form of a series of small lakes which have become such a feature of the local landscape. Much land is restored to agriculture on the completion of quarrying but inevitably land surface levels are somewhat lowered. At present active quarrying occupies a large area of the Postern but within a few years extraction here is expected to cease and new production may commence further downstream. Brief details of gravel working areas are included below.

Haysden Water (C23) in 2003. The Medway Viaduct on the A21 bypass runs overhead.

C23 Former gravel working ★
Haysden Water 560457

Haysden Water, used for small boat sailing, was a gravel extraction site in the 1970s. With another lake to its west, it was worked by Redlands. See photograph above.

C24 Ballast pit ★
Haysden 573459

A water-filled pit 300 yards in length lies alongside the railway tracks at Haysden Country Park, marking where ballast was extracted for building the railway in the 1840s. (Ballast forms the bed of stones that supports the track.) The Ballast Pit was formerly popular for swimming and skating but is now reserved for anglers.

C25 Former gravel working ★
Barden Lake 574461

Barden Lake, now part of the Haysden Country Park, was a gravel extraction site worked by Redland between 1974 and 80. The average thickness of the gravel deposit was 12ft, topped by 'overburden' of 6 ft. Extraction was by dragline excavator, with the processing plant sited at Haysden.

C26 Former gravel working ★
Hawden 575470

This area west of the mainline railway, north of the Medway bridge, was worked by RMC Ltd between 1982 and 87. It was then restored with a lake and island, for nature conservation and surrounding pasture.

C27, C28 Gravel workings ★
Postern area 607471

Despite strong local opposition, RMC Ltd began extraction at this large site in 1987 and was due to complete it in about 2002, but the term has been extended. The site is reached by a private road from Hadlow Road, including a bridge over the Medway. Sand is a major constituent of the 100,000 tons extracted annually. Half the site will eventually be returned to agricultural use, and half landscaped for conservation purposes.

D   Metalworking and engineering

Evidence of a small cutlery-making industry in the local area between 1550 and 1620 has been found by Chalklin. Its scale is uncertain, but it was enough to lead one writer of the time to refer to 'Tonbridge, where fine knives are made'. There was also a bell-foundry, owned by Giles Reeve, in the town at about this time.

Blacksmiths would have been a feature of the town community from its earliest days. There were seven blacksmiths at work in the town in the 1660s; by 1881 there were five forges in the town and 30 men working as blacksmiths, according to that year's census. In addition there were 14 foundry workers, 14 coach workers, 13 wheelwrights and 3 engineers. The 20th century brought general engineering workshops, cycle workshops and motor engineers, some of whom, such as Ravilious at 6 Shipbourne Road, evolved from earlier coachmaking and wheelwrights' businesses. (For information about the Wealden iron industry see B6-B9 and page 38).

Advertisement for Gray Brothers' foundry in Kelly's Directory of Kent, 1882.

**GRAY BROS.,
IRON AND BRASS FOUNDERS,
ENGINEERS, SPRING MANUFACTURERS,
MACHINISTS, MILLWRIGHTS, TIRE AND GENERAL SMITHS.
TUNBRIDGE.**
Close to the Down Side of the S.E.R. Station.
PARK AND OTHER IRON FENCING.
Castings for Builders, Engineers, and Agriculturalists to any extent and weight required.
AGRICULTURAL IMPLEMENTS SUPPLIED TO ORDER, MADE, OR REPAIRED.

D1   Smithy   ★
Portman Park / Shipbourne Road   592471

George Coules was the blacksmith at 1 Portman Park, now 'The Cottage', in the 1880s, though by 1909 the smithy had moved to 8 Shipbourne Road, now World of Pots, and was run by the Coules brothers. William Wenham was 'shoeing smith' there in 1929 but by the start of World War 2 the smithy had closed.

D2   Smithy   ●
High Street / Avebury Avenue   588461

The Waghorn family carried on their farrier's business in the High Street, where Avebury Avenue is now. They moved to a new site in Avebury Avenue when the High Street was widened in the 1890s and were still in business in the 1960s.

W. Waghorn, smith and farrier, at their High Street site in c.1890 — see D2. (THS 14A/402)

D3 Smithy

Great Bridge/East Street 591466

Nicholas John Drury, blacksmith, had premises near the Great Bridge and at 7 East Street in the 1880s. Twenty years later Frank Drury was the blacksmith, now operating at 12 East Street, behind the Man of Kent pub. He was followed by Osborne Allen who was later joined by his son. By 1948 the younger Allen had moved, with the forge, to Lyons Crescent (see D7).

D4 Foundry

Botany 590463

The name of Seale (or Seale and Austen or Seale, Austen and Barnes) can be found on numerous manhole and drain covers along the town's older (pre-Second World War) roads and wider afield, and also on older lamp-posts where these remain.

There was an ironmonger's shop on the corner of New Wharf Road and the High Street in the 1830s, whose proprietor, by 1859, was John Seale. He was succeeded by his wife, Anne, and son, James. Seale and Son's iron and brass foundry was behind the shop, but had moved to new premises described as the Botany Bay Ironworks by 1882. Following amalgamation with other foundries, the firm became Seale and Austen in 1898 and Seale, Austen and Barnes in 1904. The foundry remained on Botany until the mid-1930s when the Ritz cinema was built on the site (G13). It supplied more than just local needs, since its products in 1899 included gas lamp columns for London and electric-light reflectors for export to Ceylon. The shop at 76/78 High Street was rebuilt when the High Street was widened and remained there until the 1940s, when it became Hammond and Hussey, ironmongers.

Cast iron cover by Seale and Austen in Church Lane, c.1900 — see D4.

D5 Foundry

High Street/Avebury Avenue 588461

Gray Brothers ironfoundry stood on the site now occupied by the Adult Education Centre. It left a lasting mark on the town in the form of the railings which adorn the Great Bridge and the Little Bridge — see photo on next page. The firm began as wheelwrights in the 1870s before developing into a general engineer,

The 'Tonbridge' kitchen range was sold, and perhaps manufactured, by Seale, Austen and Barnes. (From an advertising handbill in THS Archives, early 20th C.)

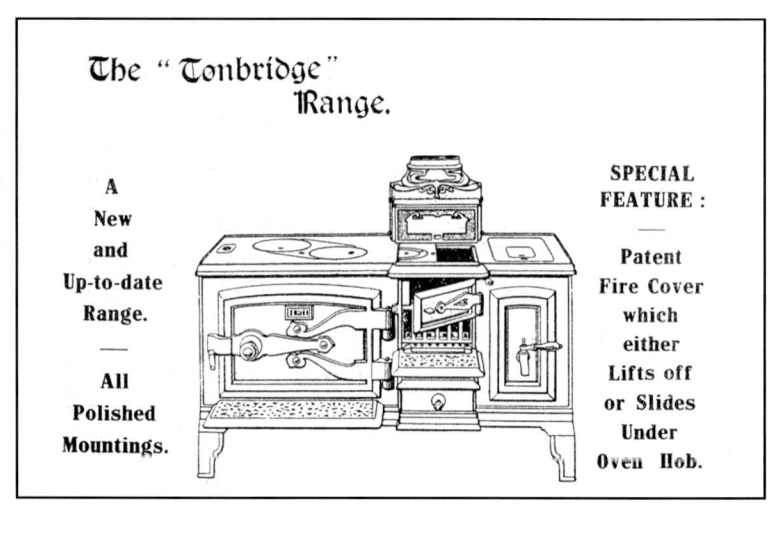

The "Tonbridge" Range.

A New and Up-to-date Range.

All Polished Mountings.

SPECIAL FEATURE:

Patent Fire Cover which either Lifts off or Slides Under Oven Hob.

D   Metalworking and engineering

millwright and iron and brass founder. It had gone by 1919.

D5

D6   Engineering works   ★
20 East Street   592466

J. T. Goodland set up his engineering business in 1919 in a workshop originally built by the Wise family (see E1) alongside the Fosse on the north side of East Street, later used as a blacksmith and wheelwright's. J. T. Goodland and Sons did engineering work for numerous firms throughout the town and also ran a garage and filling station on the site. This moved to premises adjacent to 5 Hadlow Road in the early 1930s. Dennis Goodland moved the engineering works in the late 1960s into a building adjacent to the present Halford's store in Cannon Lane, which had previously been the Test House where Patterson Candy Ltd, successor to British Berkefeld Filters (see E14) tested the large filters they supplied for waterworks. The firm, now Goodland Engineering Ltd, remains on this site. The East Street building remains, but the Hadlow Road site is now a block of flats.

D7   Engineering works   ★
Lyons Crescent / N. bank of R. Medway   592464

The premises that now houses the motor repair and servicing business of R. Allen (Tonbridge) Ltd., sandwiched between modern riverside developments in Lyons Crescent, was erected in the early 1900s. A variety of trades was carried out there over the years by a Mr Powell, later by Messrs Allen and Ashby, and since 1946 by Henry Welch and his sons. These included blacksmith (there is still a disused forge on the site), a livery stable, repair of carts and wagons, carpentry, bicycle sales and repairs, gas engine servicing, precision engineering, welding, and agricultural and motor engineering.

D7   (THS 4/162)

D8   Omnibus Depot   ●
Corner of Avebury Avenue and Holford Street   586461

A bus garage of considerable size stood in Avebury Avenue, with a back entrance on Barden Road. Opened by Redcar in the mid-1920s, by 1927 it employed over 100 men in a well-equipped workshop. Albion, Dennis and Talbot Buses were maintained and re-sprayed here, on premises where, according to a 1927 report, 'washing has recently been speeded up and improved by the installation of a B.E.N.-Myers pressure washing plant'. The depot was acquired by Maidstone and District in 1935 and later demolished. Enterprise House now occupies the site. Later a bus garage stood on the corner of Pembury Road and Quarry Hill Road (now Tonbridge Chambers).

E Manufacturing

Pigot's Directory of 1839 lists Tonbridge's manufactures as gunpowder (see B4) and 'the celebrated Tunbridge Ware' (E1), these being the only items produced to serve markets beyond the immediate area. (The manufacturing of goods for purely local consumption, such as clothing and leather goods, had of course gone on in the town for many years.) Later in the 19th century the manufacture of cricket balls became an important local industry (E2-E3), and large-scale printing flourished from the turn of the 20th (E8-E10). At this time also, the industrial estates began to take shape, centered round the Town Mills at one end of the town and on the former Walter's Farm estate at the other (E11-E22). By the 1960s the town's products included water filtration equipment, lighter flints, sheepskin goods, tar derivatives, precast concrete and fibre-glass, plastics mouldings, electrical components, and many others.

Tunbridge Ware

In 1847 Tunbridge Ware was described as the 'only manufacture of consequence' established in Tonbridge town. The ware is usually associated with Tunbridge Wells, but there is good reason to suggest it originated in Tonbridge. The term was used in the late 18th century to describe woodware made as a sideline by local woodworkers for sale to the many visitors thronging to the Wells. Specialist manufacturers started

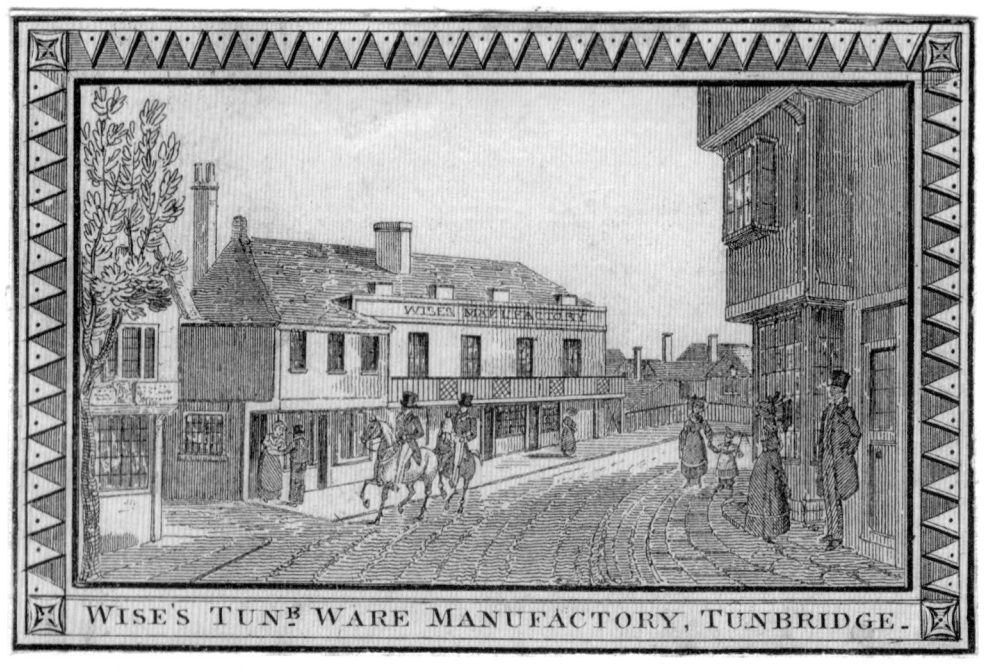

Wise's Tunbridge Ware Manufactory, in an engraving used to decorate some of their products, early 19th century — see E1. Part of the Chequers Inn appears on the right. (THS 14B/214)

E   Manufacturing

work in the mid-18th century, of whom the Burrows family in Tunbridge Wells and the Wises in Tonbridge (E1) are the most notable. By 1800 Tunbridge Ware often took the form of whitewood objects carrying printed labels depicting local scenes. The distinctive mosaic style, made by glueing sticks of different woods side by side and then slicing it into layers, came in the mid 19th century, and it is this form that is now generally understood by the term 'Tunbridge Ware'. In 1840 there was just the one manufacturer in Tonbridge, against nine in the Tunbridge Wells area, though only one of these survived beyond 1903.

E1   Wise's Manufactory   •
High Street   590465

George Wise, a turner, (1703-79) is known to have had a business in the town in 1746 at a time when the navigation of the Medway opened up greater markets for trade. With his son Thomas (1750-1807), also in the firm, he advertised Tunbridge Ware as one of their products in 1784. The workshop stood at the North end of the Big Bridge on the East side, and was originally leased, but Thomas Wise bought the premises in 1804. It had convenient river frontage and room for storage, workshops, residence for the family and showrooms. The woodworking firm gradually developed a specialisation in Tunbridge Ware and print publishing. Thomas' nephew George (1779-1869) took over in 1806, consolidating their reputation for workboxes, tea caddies, games etc, made in whitewood with prints of places like Tunbridge Wells and Brighton attached. Wise's Tonbridge business flourished and in the 1830s a retail branch was opened in Tunbridge Wells in Calverley Promenade (now Calverley Park Crescent) and in the Pantiles in 1845. The firm also opened another workshop in the Wells. George's son, George (1816-99) carried on the work until 1876. The Tonbridge premises were demolished in 1886, to widen the approach to the Bridge.

From 1856-70 George Wise junior also had premises at 59 High Street, a narrow frontage adjacent to the present Woolworth's. Thomas Burrows carried on a Tunbridge Ware business there until the late 1880s.

Cricket Ball making

The area round Tonbridge has been associated with the making of cricket bats and balls since the eighteenth century. Villages such as Penshurst and Chiddingstone and the town of Southborough all had flourishing workshops in the 19th century and Tonbridge joined the trend in the 1870s. The Census of 1881 lists 252 cricket ball makers in the whole country, of whom 178 (71%) lived in the Tonbridge area, 47 of them in the town itself. The industry depended on tanning for supply of the leather, and required similar skills to saddle-making. It is said to have flourished here because local water was good for tanning. Ball-making was essentially a craft, with most of the work done by hand, and only a little by machine.

Charles Smith and Thomas Ives became partners in a ball factory in the back of Ives's house in Baltic Road in 1875, moving a few years later into a workshop in nearby Woodlands Road. Another ball maker was Thomas Kingswood whose family business was set up by the Big Bridge in 1882.

By 1896 Smith and Ives had outgrown their premises and built a bigger three-storey workshop on the corner of Baltic road (E2). When this was taken over by John Wisden of London, Ives broke away and set up his own works at the end of Preston Road in 1897 (E3). At this point a trade union, The Amalgamated Society of Cricket

Ball Makers was formed with its registered office in the Mitre Hotel, Hadlow Road, and later in the Station Tavern in the High Street. By 1900 a third workshop, the Kent Cricket and Football Manufacturing Company, later owned by Duke & Son of Penshurst, was established by the Big Bridge. Soon after this G. W. Frowd came to the town to open a Lillywhite Frowd ball factory at the Riverside Works on the north side of the river, between the Big Bridge and Lyons Wharf.

By the 1920s the industry was flourishing and the 240 craftsmen were jealous of the secrets of the process to such an extent that apprentices were forbidden to see the final stages of the work. In 1923 the union was recreated as the English Cricket Ball Manufacturers' Association with its meetings held at the Angel Hotel. One of their concerns in this decade was the setting up of a manufacturing commune in the old skating rink (see G15) where some workers were employed full-time and others 'moonlighted' from their normal jobs. However, pressure from the employers caused it to collapse.

In 1932 Gradidge set up a small ball workshop in the upper room of 149a High Street, on the corner of East Street, and in 1938 Stuart Sturridge opened a ball factory at Salford Terrace, 19 Quarry Hill Road (later White's Pianos). In the same year Lillywhite Frowd opened another ball making works in Bradford Street. Two other firms, the Harlequin Ball and Sports Company in Priory Street and the Games Ball Company were operating at this time. There was plenty of business as the industry supplied balls to the services and schools in addition to the Test and County games.

The market diminished after World War 2, partly because colonial countries developed their own cricket ball industries. In 1951 the Riverside works of Lillywhite Frowd was demolished and the firm moved to the former home of the manager of the gasworks in Medway Wharf Road; the house was converted into a workshop and used until 1968, but has since been demolished. In 1961 Surridge from Salford Terrace and Ives from Preston Road moved their ball making to Chiddingstone as part of a larger concern known as Tonbridge Sports Industries which also included Wisden, Duke and Sons, Gray Nicholls and Twort and Sons. In 1965 this successful amalgamation was handling half the country's market, still making by hand and by the end of the decade employing more women. At one stage its 23 workers were turning out 30,000 balls a year, including every one used in Test Matches. The next decade saw the end of the industry in Tonbridge town, though ball-making continued at Chiddingstone until 1994.

E2   Cricket Ball factory   ★

5 Baltic Road   585452

This three-storey factory was built in 1896 to house the cricket ball factory of Charles Smith and Thomas Ives, formerly in Woodlands Road. It housed 70 craftsmen and was lit by oil lamps hung from the ceiling on long wires. The factory was soon taken over by the sports shop of John Wisden (of 'Almanac' fame) in London, who was placing large orders with the

E   Manufacturing

business. A wing was later added to make the present L-shaped building. Smith stayed on in the new firm but Ives broke away to set up a new enterprise (E3).

The factory was doing badly in the late 1930s and in 1939 was requisitioned as a Civil Defence Centre and later for use by the RAF. It was revived after the war as a cricket ball factory by the Co-operative Society of Manchester and continued to operate until 1961. Wisden had amalgamated with Duke and Son of Penshurst in 1920, and work continued at the firm's Chiddingstone site, later Tonbridge Sports Industries. The Baltic Road building is now occupied by a manufacturer of prescription lenses.

E3   Cricket Ball factory   ★
30 Preston Road   584461

Thomas Ives built this two-storey factory in 1897. He had split from his former partner Charles Smith after their original firm was taken over by John Wisden of London. The new firm was supposed to work solely for Wisden and when Smith disobeyed this ruling, Ives left. His Preston Road factory employed up to 70 craftsmen and also gave stitching and seaming work to outworkers. 40,000 balls a year were being produced in the 1950s, one third of them for export.

Bat-making started in 1960 after Ives took over an Essex batmaker. Ball-making ceased on this site in the following year on the formation of Tonbridge Sports Industries and the craftsmen moved to Chiddingstone. Beverly Ives, the fourth generation in the business, was manager there in the 1960s. In 1971 a fire destroyed the interior of the Preston Road factory and the bat-makers moved temporarily to Chiddingstone also. The building now houses a specialist firm making plastic injection moulds.

Printing

For a century before Tonbridge began to earn its reputation as an important printing centre, it supported (like most small towns at the time) a number of small jobbing printers (E4-E7) working in High Street premises to meet local needs for handbills, programmes, timetables, business stationery and much else. None of the original firms survives, though others have sprung up using modern techniques to meet a similar demand. A local newspaper was also printed in the town from 1869 to 1965 (E6).

Large-scale printing began in the town in the 1890s, when the first of two London firms set up its 'country' branch here (E8, E9). Like other London printers at that time they were seeking

Like many Victorian printers, Bridger's (see E4) ran a sideline in patent medicines bearing labels printed on their own press. H. S. Bridger (Harry) was in charge in the 1880s. (THS archives)

more space and lower wages and overheads. Both firms prospered, and were joined by a third (E10) until the industry eventually employed about 1000 people in the town. The Crystalate Company (see E12) also ran its own printing works in Mill Crescent for a while. All four firms have now gone.

E4 Printer ★
163 High Street 591468

William Bridger set up the family business when be took over the print works of Thomas Dakin at 131 The Terrace (later 163 High Street) in 1830. By the 1840s his services included printer and bookseller, news vendor and binder. In 1856 Fred Bridger was in charge, followed by other members of the family, right up to 1967. The premises then became a book shop and are now a restaurant.

E5 Printer ★
129-131 High Street 590466

In 1856 William Ware, postmaster, ran a printing and stationery business at the Post Office, next to the Rose & Crown. Richard Ware was running it in 1862 and the premises had split into Nos. 101 and 103 High Street (now 129 and 131) by 1884. Ware's business was taken over by Stonestreet (E7) in 1887, at which time Blair and Twort's Tonbridge Free Press (E6) moved in.

E6 Printer/Newspaper Office ★
129-131 High Street 590466

William Blair launched the *Tonbridge Free Press* in 1869 with an office in the High Street which soon moved to the corner of Medway Wharf Road (see photograph on page 20), on the site now occupied by the Castle Hotel, where it remained until displaced by road widening in 1887. The printing press was in a loft of the White Hart Inn yard, now Blair House, 184-6 High Street. In 1887 the business moved to 103 (later 129) High Street where it occupied the former premises of Richard Ware (E5). The stationer's shop was in the front and the composing and printing works at the rear of the building.

In 1900 the firm, now known as Blair & Twort, replaced its old hand presses with a machine press, albeit powered by two brawny men until they were replaced by a gas engine. More improvements were made in 1924 and it was not until 1965 that the printing was transferred to Maidstone. The *Tonbridge Free Press* celebrated its centenary in 1969 but ceased publication soon after, and the High Street office finally closed in 1970. The building, with altered frontage, now houses an Estate Agent and a Building Society.

E7 Printer ★
25 High Street 589462

Manesseh Stonestreet took over Ware's printing business (E5) in c.1887 and moved it to 25 High Street, where it lasted as a family business until c.1937. Stonestreet was a printer and bookbinder, stationer and newsagent, and for a time housed the offices of the *Tonbridge Telegraph* newspaper. The premises had rear access to the Angel Cricket Ground (G16) enabling Stonestreet's to print and sell up-to-the-minute scorecards on the Ground. The premises now house a shoe repair business.

Billhead used by Stonestreet's in the 1890s – see E7. (THS archives)

25, HIGH STREET, TONBRIDGE, _____ 189
(Near the Little Bridge).

Dr. to M. STONESTREET,
(Successor to the late R. WARE).

Letter-Press, Copper-Plate, & Lithographic Printer.
STATIONER, BOOKBINDER, AND NEWSAGENT.

Business & Commercial Printing. Auctioneers' Work. Price Lists. Circulars. Hand Bills.
Balance Sheets. Special attention given to Friendly Societies' requirements, &c., &c.

E   Manufacturing

Whitefriars Press from the south-west. The original warehouse is left of centre. (Bradbury, Agnew promotional booklet, pre-1916)

E8   The Whitefriars Press ●
Medway Wharf Road   592464

The Whitefriars Press was Tonbridge's largest employer in its day. The firm was founded in the 1820s when William Bradbury took over an earlier printing business in Bouverie Street in the Whitefriars district of London. In 1841 he purchased the right to print and publish the newly-established 'Punch' magazine.

By 1896 the firm, by now called Bradbury and Agnew, wanted to set up a country printing works, and settled on a three-floor former warehouse in Medway Wharf Road. Here they installed a book composing room (where type was set), a jobbing composing room, a machine room (where the printing was done), and a bindery, employing about 100 people in all. Gas engines powered the machinery, running on the town gas supply, and also drove dynamos for electric lighting.

Book production began, using paper brought up by barge from the Medway towns, and new buildings were soon added adjacent to the original one as work expanded. The premises eventually occupied more than an acre. All typesetting was done by hand until the first mechanical system, the Typograph, was introduced in about 1909, followed later by Monotype machines. The Whitefriars Press Club and Institute was established in Lansdowne Road in c.1907.

Bradbury and Agnew sold their Tonbridge works to the Standard Catalogue Company in 1916, at which point it became The Whitefriars Press Ltd. A catastrophic fire made national headlines in 1926 and destroyed half the factory, but allowed the firm to rebuild and re-equip the works as an up-to-date printing establishment. By the late 1940s Whitefriars, with 300-350 employees, was specialising in high-class multi-colour work, catalogues, and book production of every description. Up to two million Penguin books a year were coming from the press in the 1950s.

Typesetters at work in the main composing room at Whitefriars. (Bradbury, Agnew promotional booklet, pre-1916)

In 1989 Whitefriars fell victim to 'restructuring' within Robert Maxwell's British Printing and Communications Corporation of which it was then part. The Medway Wharf Road site was closed and its functions transferred elsewhere. The typesetting operation moved to Tunbridge Wells, where it became part of the Polestar Group, a large independent printing group.

The Whitefriars Wharf housing development was built on the site of the former printing works in 2003-4.

E9   The Dowgate Press   ●
Douglas Road   582459

The second large printing firm in the town began modestly when the City printer James Truscott and Son started a small bindery in the former Christ Church building in Lansdowne Road (since demolished) in 1899. The firm had been started before 1850 by the Cornishman James Truscott, whose son Francis became alderman for the Dowgate Ward of the City of London and later Lord Mayor.

Work on the new Dowgate Works in the Meadow Lawn area of Tonbridge began in 1900 and there were several subsequent expansions. About 250 people were employed there in 1937, when Truscott and Son amalgamated with two other famous London printers to form Brown, Knight and Truscott. Charles Knight had been a writer as well as a printer and publisher in early Victorian times, and a friend of Charles Dickens. His company patented the idea of printing from colour blocks in 1838, and claims to have been the first in Britain to print by steam power.

The third partner, William Brown, had helped establish a print works in Old Broad Street in 1815, specialising in the production of cheques and stationery.

The Tonbridge works was extended and modernised after an air raid in 1941 had totally destroyed one of the firm's London sites, whose work was then transferred to Tonbridge. The Dowgate Works eventually covered 2.5 acres. In the late 1940s the firm's output included high-class colour printing in letterpress and by lithography, and the production of cheques, account books and other stationery. They also ran a Social and Sports Club in the Burton's building in the High Street. The firm's name, blazoned on the factory roof, became a landmark for travellers arriving by train from Redhill or London.

The Dowgate site was sold in 1988. Brown, Knight and Truscott moved to purpose-built accommodation in Tunbridge Wells, where they remain. Nothing is left of the Tonbridge works, whose site is now occupied by new housing in Amberley Close and Arundel Close.

E10   Tonbridge Printers   ●
Trench Road   593485

Tonbridge Printers started as a co-operative in 1921, with its premises at the rear of the *Good Intent* in Waterloo Road. In 1923 it moved to the Peach Hall works, behind what is now Peter Newman's shoe shop.

In 1930 it moved again to the old Little Trench Farm buildings in Shipbourne Road and in 1932 was taken over by a London firm. More than a million books a year were being produced in the mid-1950s, along with periodicals, diaries and other items. The firm remained until the 1980s. Trenchwood Medical Centre now occupies the site.

Clocking-off time at the Dowgate Works in 1966 (Courier photo 98397)

E   Manufacturing

The Industrial Estate

Tonbridge's main industrial area, on the eastern side of the town, began to develop in the early part of the twentieth century. At the south end, development took place on the Walter's Farm site. The farm itself stood on what is now the site of the Royal Mail sorting office. It was reached by a track, Walter's Farm Road, which was an extension of Medway Wharf Road and can still be followed today as a public bridleway. A spur from this road led north into the 19th-C municipal sewage works (see F11). Vale Road, laid out alongside the railway, was eventually extended to link up with Walter's Farm Road. Several of the firms that set up in this area were involved with chemicals.

At the north end, development spread from the Town Mills site (B1) down to the Medway, on both sides of Postern Lane, which then ran as an extension of Mill Lane to the narrow Cannon Bridge and beyond. Part of it later became Cannon Lane. There were also a number of industrial concerns on the low-lying ground between Lyons Crescent and the river.

The planned connection between the two main industrial areas, Cannon Lane and Vale Road, was achieved in the 1970s by the replacement of the narrow Cannon Lane bridge (H6). Before the contract was let the 1968 flood demolished the old bridge, and at the request of the Kent River Authority the clear waterway was increased from the planned 90 feet to 120 feet. With the completion of the Leigh Flood Barrier the risk of flooding was reduced, allowing rapid development along the new road, known locally as the 'mini-bypass'.

Gazetteer entries are given, in order of arrival, for the principal firms that set up in the area before 1950.

Advertisement for the celebrated Acme weed killer, in 'Tonbridge and District', by W. S. Martin, 1896

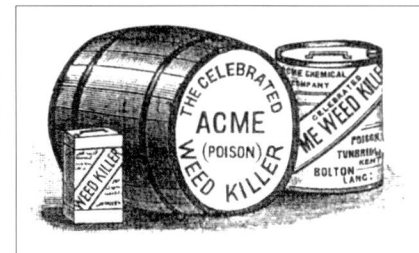

For Destroying Weeds, Moss, &c., on Carriage Drives, Garden Walks, Roads, Stable Yards, Walls, Stonework, &c.

E11   The Acme Chemical Company Ltd   ●

Vale Road   596459

H. A. Grindrod set up his Agri-Horticultural Chemical Co. in St Stephens Street in the late 1880s. By 1896 it had become the Acme Chemical Co. Ltd., and was manufacturing the 'Celebrated Acme Weedkiller', claimed to keep 'Walks and Drives clear of Weeds for at least eighteen months' with a single application. In the early years of the new century the company expanded to a larger site backing the railway at the east end of Vale Road.

Grindrod was still the manager in 1929, by which time the company's product range had expanded to include worm killer, hopwash, and a range of fertilizers and insecticides. The company is listed in Kelly's Directory for 1939, but vanished soon after. In 1948 its premises were occupied by Sheepskin Utilities Ltd (E18). The location, formerly allotments, now forms the small Riverdale Estate.

E12   The Crystalate Company   ●

Cannon Lane   596468

The Crystalate Company was making billiard balls at its works in Three Elm Lane at Golden Green in 1902, in premises formerly occupied by the Mid Kent Jam Company. 'Crystalate' was the name of the composite material used. Manufacture of gramophone records probably began a few years later, when Crystalate took over from a short-lived venture called 'Neophone' which attempted to produce 'indestructible' gramophone records from papier maché. Crystalate's 'Town Works' in Tonbridge opened in 1917 pressing 78 r.p.m. records made of shellac – the sticky secretions of an Asian insect, mixed with fine clay or other filler. The manager was W. C. Chalklin, and there were 40 employees.

The Crystalate Gramophone Record Manufacturing Company grew into a major provider of popular music on disc, producing millions of records under its Imperial, Eclipse, and Rex labels. By 1933 the firm had some 400 employees working in its two large buildings located where the Homebase store now stands in Cannon Lane. Crystalate also ran a printing works nearby, and had offices at Crystalate House, the former convent in Mill Crescent now replaced by Shrublands Court.

By 1937 the Company's record making business was in trouble. Crystalate was trying to undercut the market by selling its Rex label discs at 1/-, compared to the 1/6d charged by Decca, HMV and Columbia, and were also supplying records for sale at 6d each in Woolworths. In March, Decca bought the Crystalate plant, trademarks and goodwill for £200,000 and transferred the record manufacturing to its existing factory in New Malden, Surrey. One employee who transferred from Crystalate to Decca was chief engineer Arthur Haddy whose team developed the 'ffrr' (full frequency range recording) system introduced in 1944, which was an important step on the road to 'high fidelity'.

Crystalate continued in the business of making plastic moulded components. Part of the Cannon Lane premises were used for a sister company, Mica Products Ltd. The Tonbridge works was damaged by fire and floods in 1968 and eventually became a garage before being demolished to make way for the link road through to Hadlow Road. The Golden Green premises had been damaged by fire in 1969. Snooker and billiard balls bearing the name 'Crystalate' are still obtainable.

E13   The Storey Motor Company ●
Cannon Lane   595466

Storey Motors was a short-lived venture to manufacture upmarket cars in Tonbridge. Jack and Will Storey ran the successful Storey Machine Tool Company at New Cross in London. In 1919 they decided to take advantage of a brief post-war boom to enter the car manufacturing business. Jack Storey bought a large site in the flood plain from the Urban District Council for £3000 and built a substantial factory there, on the site now occupied by Halfords and B&Q. A work-force was recruited by offering high wages, and manufacture began. Products included a 20 h.p. saloon, the 'Tonbridge', which sold for £1200, and a number of smaller models.

By late 1920 several hundred Storey cars had been built, but an industrial slump forced the venture into liquidation, and the Storey brothers retreated back to London.

E14   Slack and Brownlow Ltd/ ★
British Berkefeld Filters
Mill Lane   595466

Slack and Brownlow Ltd began making water filters in Manchester in the mid 19th century, and later set up British Berkefeld Filters. The principal product was a water purifier

The former Storey Motors works, with the gasworks beyond, photographed during a flood, date unknown. (THS 17/16)

consisting of a large jar with a tap at the bottom. Impure water poured in at the top emerged pure from the tap, having passed through a ceramic filter on the way. In hot climates the filter was described as a 'necessity for the health of the population' and 'a safeguard against cholera, typhoid and kindred water borne diseases'. In 1921 Slack and Brownlow moved south to be nearer to London Docks, since much of their output was for export, and acquired the former Storey Motors factory (E13) from the liquidators. A group of bottle-shaped kilns, for firing the porous pot used in the filters, could be seen near the Mill bridge until the 1960s. Some 200 people worked for the firm, producing filters and water softeners of various sizes, and other products such as hot water bottles. It was later taken over by Patterson Engineering (later Patterson Candy).

The factory was on the site now occupied by B&Q and Halfords and their car parks, but the only remaining parts are the Test House, now partially re-clad and occupied by Goodland Engineering (D6), and some other small outbuildings. Royal Doulton acquired the British Berkefeld Filters name in 1985 and the filter, little changed from the original product, is still produced today, though not in Tonbridge.

E15   South-Eastern Tar Distillers Ltd ●

Vale Road   598460

In 1928, existing tar distillers from London and Birmingham set up a co-operative with gasworks in Kent, Surrey and Sussex to process the crude tar that they produced as part of the gas-making process. Tonbridge was chosen as a convenient distribution centre, and tankers went out from the large Vale Road depot to gasworks throughout the three counties. Crude tar was brought back and treated to produce a range of products that included road tar, creosote and naphthalene (used as a fumigant by farmers). Large quantities of road tar were exported from here in the years after the World War 2 to help rebuild the crippled road system on the continent. By then the tar industry's products were making a valuable contribution to the national economy by also providing raw materials for the plastics, dyestuffs, explosives and paint industries.

In 1953 plant for distilling crude benzole was added, its products including Benzole motor spirit and paint solvents. By the mid-1950s 14 million gallons of crude tar and 2.5 million gallons of Benzole a year were being distilled on the site. Some 40 further chemicals, including anaesthetics and other pharmaceuticals, were produced.

From the late 1930s part of the site was a depot for Johnson Bros., road contractors.

The SETAR site passed to Colas Roads and remained in their hands until its closure in the 1990s, remaining derelict until 2004 when it was decontaminated ready for redevelopment. Colas (short for 'Cold Asphalt') had been formed in 1929 to exploit a new road-surfacing process invented by two British chemists. It is now a multinational involved in road building in many parts of the world.

E16   G. E. Mortley Sprague and Co. Ltd ●

Lyons Crescent   593465

The firm was founded by G. E. Mortley in Tunbridge Wells in 1913 to exploit his various patents and inventions. These included motor-cycle dynamos, and electrical generators to power radios in World War 1 aircraft.

Walter Sprague became Mortley's partner in 1921, bringing business and management skills to complement Mortley's inventiveness. The Tonbridge factory was built in 1942 to provide more manufacturing space. In World War 2 Mortley Sprague again supplied generators for military aircraft, and also pedal-powered generators for Aldis lamps on landing beaches. The firm then diversified into quality electronic and electro mechanical subcontracting, manufacturing equipment for the aerospace and environmental industries, among others. The Lyons Crescent factory was vacated in the 1990s and has since been demolished to make way for housing. Mortley Close now marks the site. Mortley Sprague later had premises in Cannon Lane, and a factory near Arundel, but closed down in 2004.

E17   E.C.D. Ltd/Wallace & Tiernan ★

Cannon Lane/Tudeley Lane   595467/601455

The Electro Chemical Development Syndicate Ltd (E.C.D.) began operations in 1932, making water purification equipment and high-accuracy metering pumps, used for inserting ingredients in precisely measured quantities in chemical processes. The firm originally occupied a building alongside the Mill Stream that had previously been part of the Town Mills, but moved to a new site at Priory Mill, off Tudeley Lane, in 1935. In the mid-50s E.C.D. was acquired by Wallace and Tiernan Ltd.

Charles Wallace and Martin Tiernan were two Americans who pioneered the use of chlorine for sterilising drinking water and other water supplies. They founded their company in New Jersey in 1913, and set up a British subsidiary in London in 1926. By the 1950s further expansion was necessary, and the acquisition of E.C.D. Ltd in Tonbridge provided a site with plenty of spare land. Wallace and Tiernan's substantial new factory was fully operational by 1963 and the firm became a major employer in the town with over 600 staff engaged, mainly, in the production of chlorination equipment. By 2002 the firm had become part of the global US Filter Corporation, USFilter. Operations at the Tonbridge factory had been scaled down and many of the 1960s buildings at the Priory Mill site were no longer in use.

E18   Sheepskin Utilities Ltd/ •
Barr, Lamb Ltd

Vale Road　　　　　　　　　　　596459

Sheepskin Utilities started in London in 1932 and came to Tonbridge ten years later. Their war-time products included thermo-insulated sheepskin worn by airmen at high altitudes and by seamen on the Russian convoys. They also cleaned 1000 army blankets daily.

After the war, raw sheepskins were imported from New Zealand, South America and elsewhere, and were tanned, dyed, stretched and dried before being made into products such as rugs, dusters and powder puffs. Half the output was exported. A staff of 121 in 1947 dwindled to only 21 as a result of the 125% purchase tax on luxury goods and competition from Germany where labour costs were half those in Britain.

Merger with another London firm brought a change of name to Barr, Lamb Ltd in 1954. It was still listed in the 1974 edition of Kelly's Directory, but the site, the former Acme Chemical works in Vale Road (E11) is now the Riverdale Estate.

E19   The Distiller's Company Ltd •

Walter's Farm Road　　　　　　　597460

In 1934 the Distiller's Company decided to set up a research station in Tonbridge. The company had long been in the business of supplying grain alcohol in the form of whisky and was now diversifying into the production of the industrial sort. The Tonbridge research station, located on the corner between Walter's Farm Road and the Botany Stream, was set up to develop the industrial alcohol process.

In 1937 the first polystyrene ever produced in Britain was synthesised on this site, and the Tonbridge plant was the sole source of this important material during World War 2. Production processes for other plastics such as PVC were developed at the station after the war, although their main manufacture took place elsewhere. In the 1960s the Tonbridge research station (officially the 'Pilot Plant Division' of the Distiller's Company) employed some 100 people, many of them research scientists. The station passed to BP Chemicals Ltd in 1967 and was closed at the end of that year as part of a restructuring programme.

E20   British Resin Products Ltd •
Vale Road　　　　　　　　　　　596461

The company listed as Honeywell and Stein Ltd., resin manufacturers, in Kelly's 1939 Directory had been renamed British Resin Products by 1947 and was a subsidiary of the Distiller's Company in Vale Road. It supplied resinous products to the plastics industry for use in insulating materials and laminated board such as Formica. 250 people were employed in 1950, when the company relocated to Barry, Glamorgan.

E21   The British Flint and •
Cerium Manufacturers Ltd

Vale Road　　　　　　　　　　　598462

British Flint and Cerium started in Ramsgate in 1928 and moved to Drayton Road in Tonbridge in 1940, transferring to the Vale Road site in 1954, where about 100 people, many of them women, were employed. Their products were cerium metal, which has specialised metallurgical uses, and lighter flints, one of whose ingredients is cerium. Flints were supplied for industrial use, for example in miners' safety lamps, and for domestic use. Flints by the million were sent all over the world from the factory, including to India, Burma, Malaya and the Dutch East Indies. The factory was still operating in the mid-70s.

E22   E. W. Tyler and Co.   •
Cannon Lane   596466

E. W. Tyler moved his company to Tonbridge from Bromley in 1948, making pre-cast concrete panels for prefabricated buildings. Kelly's 1950 Directory puts his works on the west side of Cannon Lane, but by 1953 it was on the east side where it remained, becoming Charcon Buildings Ltd. in the 1970s. With about 100 employees in 1955, the company was supplying some 500 agricultural buildings a year, such as Dutch barns and cow sheds, in addition to many bus shelters. Industrial buildings with the Tyler and Charcon nameplates can still be seen in the area.

In 1960, Tyler and his son John used their expertise with concrete to develop a process for moulding boat hulls out of glass-reinforced plastic (GRP). The business flourished on new premises adjacent to the river in Cannon Lane (597466) and there was also a boatyard at Hoo, near Rochester. By 1969, 1000 glass-fibre hulls had been completed, mainly for yachts, most of them for export. The Tyler Boat Company moved into new premises in Sovereign Close (now Morley Road) in 1973.

Production ceased after a fire in 1978, but Tyler Holdings, a property management company, maintains an office in Morley Road.

A 57-foot hull leaving the Tyler works in 1967. (THS 4/1, Courier 1490)

F Utilities and services

Gas was the first of the public utilities (as they are now known) to be established in Tonbridge, in the 1830s, and within the next 70 years the others all followed. All were dependent on developments in technology as well as on local initiative – or in the case of sewerage, the lack of it. The Gas Works (1836, see F1-F3) and Water Works (1852, F4) were started by private companies, whereas the Sewage Treatment Works (1873, F11) and Electric Light Station (1902, F14) were the responsibility of the local authority. (For the telegraph and telephone, see pages 75-77).

Among the public services, organised fire-fighting (F20-F24), based on the simple technology of bucket, hose and hand-pump, was established in the town in the mid-18th century.

Gas

Tonbridge Gas Company was established in 1836 for the purpose of lighting the streets. The first gasworks was between Medway Wharf Road and the river, at the west end of Old Cannon Wharf. Coal was delivered by barge and roasted in closed ovens to produce gas which was piped to lamps in the High Street, Bordyke and East Street. The first lighting of these, on the evening of 12th November 1836, was an occasion for public celebration. Lamplighters lit and extinguished the lamps, which were initially only used during the winter months. Gas was only produced in the evenings, and for a few days around full moon the lamps were not lit at all.

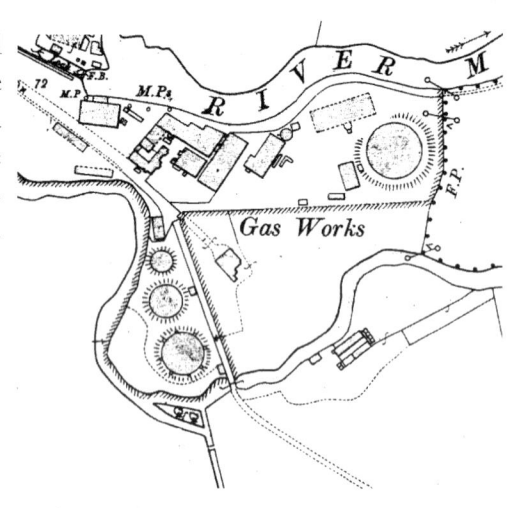

The gasworks site in 1908. The Town Lock is at the top left. The Gasworks Stream, along the south side, has now been filled in.

By 1856 the Company was supplying gas for 51 street lamps and about 150 private consumers, including Tonbridge School and the Parish Church. Street-lighting reached Priory Street, Lavender Hill and Primrose Hill in 1865, and the Pinnacles in Shipbourne Road only in 1897. Lamps were initially either of the 'Argand' or 'batswing' type, in which the light came directly from the flame itself. Incandescent mantles, which gave much brighter light, were tried out in two lamps on the Big Bridge in 1895, and subsequently widely adopted. Gas street-lamps, now converted for electricity, survive on the Big Bridge and Little Bridge in the High Street, and probably elsewhere in the town. New gas street lamps were still being installed, in

F   Utilities and services

places not yet on the electricity mains, as late as 1923, and there were still 28 gas streetlamps lamps in use in various parts of the town in 1933.

In addition to lighting, gas was also in use as an industrial power source by the 1890s, fuelling gas-powered engines that were more convenient than steam engines for smaller-scale applications. Baltic Saw Mills considered installing a 12 or 16 horsepower gas engine, and another was proposed for the new Quarry Hill brickworks. Tonbridge School installed a gas-engine in 1894 to drive its electric generator, and the *Tonbridge Free Press* later used one to replace human labour on its presses.

Dramatic growth in the use of gas for domestic cooking and heating did not come until the 20th century, by which time gas was available 24 hours a day. In 1927, for example, a record 324 cookers, 301 fires and 66 water-heaters were installed. For 100 years from 1836 demand for gas increased every year, requiring frequent enlargement of the gasworks and laying of bigger pipes. The first expansion, in 1864, was southwards, onto land between Walters Farm Road and the gasworks stream, and one building still survives on this site (see F1). Subsequent expansion was along the river bank towards Cannon Lane, and a portion of this site, including two gasholders (F2), remains in use for gas storage.

In the mid-1930s, Tonbridge Gas Company was absorbed into the South Suburban Gas Company, which in turn became the South Eastern Gas Board on nationalisation in 1949. Production of gas at the Tonbridge works ceased in the late 1960s, since when the Tonbridge installation has been a Holder Station for distributing gas piped in from Maidstone. Conversion from Towns Gas to natural gas (North Sea gas) followed a few years later.

Independent of the public supply, Somerhill had its own private gasworks (F3), and there may also have been a private gasworks for the mansion at Tonbridge Castle, since a gasometer is shown nearby on the 1866 O.S. map.

F1   Gasworks Forge   ★

Medway Wharf Road   594463

A rectangular brick building on the right of Medway Wharf Road where it becomes Walters Farm Road (No. 1 Ashby's Yard) appears to be the only remaining part of the Tonbridge Gas Company's works, apart from the gasholders. It is labelled 'Forge and Store' on a plan of 1889.

F2   Gasholders   ★

Old Cannon Wharf   595463

The smaller of the two gasholders was purchased for £4500 in 1895 and bears the maker's plate: C & W Walker, Donnington, Shropshire 1895 – a well-known firm in the gas industry.

The larger gasholder, now the most conspicuous feature of the Tonbridge skyline, is almost certainly the 950,000 cubic foot one purchased from the same supplier for £15,752 in 1922.

F3	Private gasworks	★

Somerhill estate 609453

This building, in the grounds of Electric Cottage on Five Oak Green Road, is marked 'gasworks' on a 1909 Ordnance Survey map. It still stands but the gasmaking plant has gone. Two gasholders stood to the north-east of it, and a direct cut links it to Five Oak Green Road, through which coal would have been carted in. Coke from this plant was probably used to heat Somerhill's greenhouses. A smaller building alongside housed the Somerhill Electricity Works (see F19).

Water supply

A piped public water supply in Tonbridge commenced in 1852, instigated by a small group of local businessmen who perhaps foresaw the need for a more constant supply of potable water for some of their own concerns such as brewing. Another factor seems to have been the passing of the Public Health Act in 1848 which required local water supplies to be reviewed prior to the setting-up of a Local Board. A small pumping station (F4) was opened near the New Wharf, beside the River Medway close to the castle, water being abstracted from the saturated gravels adjacent to the river and pumped to a circular reservoir high above the town close to Pembury Road. At this stage the supply is said to have reached only 176 houses, and clearly most of the town's inhabitants still relied on traditional sources. For many centuries water had been obtained from private wells, dipping places beside the various streams which flow across the locality, and a few public springs and wells. A public pump, installed by the Town Wardens beside the Great Bridge in 1793, can be seen in the print reproduced on page 28. The Wardens moved this pump to the Town Hall in the 1840s, and at some date installed another at the Little Bridge.

As the town grew in the later 19th century the area supplied from the New Wharf works also expanded, leading to further development at the works including considerable extension to the area of supply from the Medway gravels. By 1890 a much larger high level, and covered, reservoir had been constructed at Bloodshots (F5) and in 1900 another similar reservoir was opened at Hangman's Hill (F7) to improve supplies to the southern part of the town. However in the early 20th century a number of Tonbridge companies still retained their own deep boreholes, including Crystalate, Quarry Hill Brickworks, Bartram's Brewery, two local laundries, and the Acme Chemical Company.

Further large increases in public demand led to the inauguration of two deep boreholes at the waterworks, and by the 1930s almost every house in

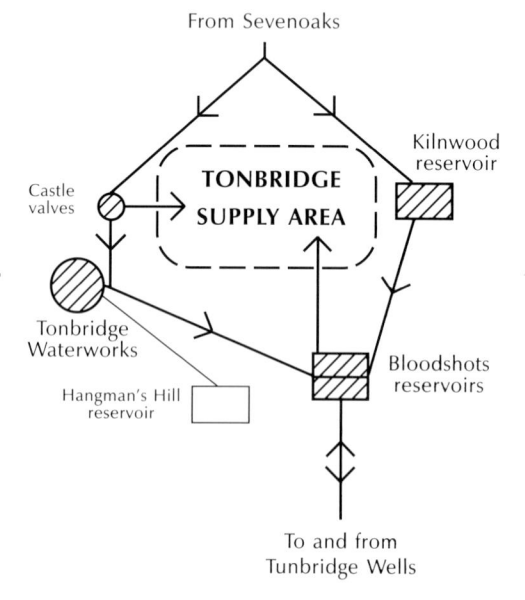

Tonbridge area water supply – see text for explanation.

F   Utilities and services

Tonbridge was connected to the mains supply. However, a decade later local sources began to prove inadequate and from about 1940 bulk supplies of water have been received from Sevenoaks sources. At present about four fifths of Tonbridge's water is pumped from boreholes at Crampton's Road in Sevenoaks and reaches Tonbridge via Riverhill and Kilnwood reservoirs.

In 1948 the Tonbridge and Sevenoaks water companies amalgamated, as part of a long sequence of mergers in this area, so that today water supply to Tonbridge, Tunbridge Wells and Sevenoaks forms a largely integrated and self-contained system with water movement taking place in numerous directions at different times according to demand. Almost all is now part of South East Water plc.

In later years a second reservoir has been built at Bloodshots and, with the now integrated system, Hangman's Hill reservoir has become disused. Further, the deeper boreholes at Tonbridge pumping station no longer pump into supply as the quality of the water has declined. Instead, they pump so called 'compensation' water into the Medway, compensating for abstraction taking place at Hartlake.

F4   Water Works   ★
New Wharf Road   588464

The Tonbridge Water Works Company set up its works on a triangular site at the north-east corner of the present waterworks, bounded by the New River Cut and New Wharf Road. A wall plaque dated 1852 (see photo F4a) and the nearby Waterworks Cottage remain from this era. The 1868 O.S. map shows three wells on the site, extracting what is essentially filtered river water from the gravel beds that lie some 15 feet under the Recreation Ground. Water was pumped by steam power to a reservoir at Bloodshots (see F5).

Subsequent expansion includes a 300-foot deep borehole drilled shortly after 1911 to tap a much deeper source, the Ashdown sands aquifer. The present Filter House (photo F4b) bears the dates 1913 and 1929, and also houses pumps. Additional plant at the enlarged works now includes settling tanks, an aeration fountain, a second borehole sunk before 1969, and a third sunk in c.2002.

F4a

F5   Reservoirs: Bloodshots   ★
S. of Pembury Road/Baltic Road   589453/588450

The town's first reservoir, supplied directly from the 1852 Water Works, was a circular tank on Bloodshots, c.220 yds south of Pembury Road, roughly where Marlfield Cottage now stands. It appears on an 1863 plan but had gone by 1897.

It was replaced by a larger reservoir higher up the hill, at the top of Deakin Lees, built in 1885. There are now two reservoirs here, constructed between 1960 and 71, with a combined capacity of 930,000 gallons.

F6   Reservoir: Kilnwood   ★
Beside A227, 0.5 m S. of Shipbourne   593511

This reservoir was constructed between 1960 and 71 and is fed from Sevenoaks via the Riverhill reservoir. Its capacity is 1,000,000 gallons.

F7 Reservoir: Hangman's Hill ★
W. of A26, S. of Mabledon   578443

Hangman's Hill lies on the A26, half a mile south of the A21 interchange. A reservoir of 140,000 gallons capacity was built here in 1900 to serve the upper Quarry Hill area, but is now disused.

F8 Gravel wells ★
Racecourse Sportsground   582465, 584467

Two black-topped circular covers on fields at the western extremity of the Sportsground show where water has been extracted, possibly since the early 20th century. They cover wells penetrating about 20 ft into the gravel layer, each fed by a network of drains. Water is pumped from here to the waterworks, via a nearby collecting chamber.

F9 Castle Valves ★
Upper Castle Field   588466

Two green boxes labelled 'Castle Valves' stand beside an undergound chamber on the footpath between the Upper Castle car park and the swimming pool. They mark an important routing point for the town's water supply, connecting the incoming flow from Sevenoaks to the waterworks and the town.

F10 Stopcock covers ★
71 & 83 Hadlow Road   597472

Small covers hide the stopcocks outside most properties in the town. The two examples shown here bear initials showing they were installed by Tonbridge Water Works Company and, after the 1948 merger, the Sevenoaks and Tonbridge Water Company respectively. Later covers simply say 'Water'.

Surface drainage and sewerage

The surface drainage net of the urban area is shown in the map on page 13 in a much simplified form. Over many years the pattern has been much altered, in particular the main stream of the river once flowed to the south under the present Little Bridge, and other water courses crossing the High Street have long been culverted. The construction of the Medway Navigation also had some major effects (see pages 86-87).

Flooding of the town centre has been a problem for a very long time. Well-remembered and disastrous floods occurred in 1880 and 1968 but there have been many inundations. In 1957 low brick flood walls and earth embankments were built along

Lyons Wharf from the Big Bridge during the 1968 flood. The white building is Lillywhite's cricket ball works. (THS 17/49)

F Utilities and services

the right bank upstream from the Town Lock. At the time these were the only protection for the High Street and other properties across this narrow section of the flood-plain, but the severe damage caused by the 1968 flood prompted much greater investment in flood control works, culminating in the building of the Leigh barrier, two miles upstream from the town (F14). Further work has since been completed in strengthening flood walls in the town centre alongside the river on both banks. They should now give protection against a storm only likely to occur once in 150 years.

Before the 19th century there was no organised system of drainage in the town and both surface and foul or waste water found its way naturally to the local streams. Not until well into the century were rudimentary efforts made at improving the town's drainage by means of open ditches leading to the Medway, for example a deep and steep channel forming an open sewer drained the High Street from the market area down to the river, and in 1832 the upper High Street, from the Chequers Inn to Church Lane, was provided with paved water channels each side of the road into which some drains from adjoining properties discharged. This work was commissioned by the Town Wardens. Nevertheless, with its increasing population and resulting new development on the Medway flood-plain the general sanitary condition of the town was not improving and was actually deteriorating.

Further initiatives by the Town Wardens and Vestry saw the construction in 1837 of the first common sewer, apparently a brick-built barrel down the High Street from the Elephant and Castle (now the Ivy House) to discharge into the Medway just below the Great Bridge. Some house drains were connected to this, and further brick sewers were built in the next three years. However, by 1854 these sewers were reported to be mostly blocked and still only a few properties were connected to them. Most houses, even then, were just drained by culverts or ditches directly to the nearest branch of the river.

Sanitation became the most important local concern in the period from 1850 to 1870 as epidemics of cholera happened repeatedly, particularly affecting the lower southern end of the town. Lack of water supply to the majority of house latrines and the casual disposal of sewage were known to be the cause, but little action was taken. An inspection of the town's sanitary condition by Mr A. L. Dickens for the General Board of Health recommended the establishment of a Local Board but this action was delayed for some fifteen years due to local opposition.

A Sewer Authority, set up in 1866, achieved little practical improvement but made the important recommendation that

One of the early brick sewers, revealed during later roadworks (THS).

the town's sewage be collected, taken to a point below the town and then treated before being released into the Medway. Finally in 1870 the Local Board was set up, with drainage as its main concern. Plans previously commissioned from Mr C. Jones of Ealing were updated and implemented. With suitable finance the new sewerage system was inaugurated and the sewage treatment works, by a branch of the River Medway, opened in 1873 (F11). This original drainage still functions today, but over the years the network has grown as the town has expanded and the treatment works has undergone much enlargement and modernisation. A sewage farm of some 15 acres was needed in the earlier years to purify the effluent but this method of treatment has long been superseded.

F11   Sewage Works   ★
Vale Road   600462

The present Wastewater Treatment Works is the third on the eastern fringe of the town. The first, opened in 1873, was on the site now occupied by a car showroom, opposite the entrance to Sanderson Way. It was upgraded with new pumps and settling tanks in 1890, and discharged into the adjacent Botany Stream branch of the Medway. The second Sewage Works opened in 1912 and was beside the railway on a site now bisected by Woodgate Way, and partially occupied by a Landrover dealership. New filter beds were added here in 1931. The present Works opened in 1965 to serve the much increased population of 45,000 at that time. It treats sewage and some storm water, and the principal outputs are sludge for agricultural use and liquid effluent clean enough to go into the Botany Stream. The Works has been considerably altered and upgraded, most recently in 2004-5.

F12   Shone Ejector   ●
Medway Wharf Road   590464

A patent device known as a Shone Ejector was installed under Medway Wharf Road, at the High Street end, in the 1890s. Its function was to raise sewage from the low level at which it collected to a higher level from which it could flow on under gravity to the Sewage Works. Sewage accumulated in an underground chamber and when this was full was automatically ejected at a higher level by the pressure of compressed air supplied from the Sewage Works.

There were two other ejectors in the town, one of them, with a vertical lift of 35 feet, being at Hilden Bridge on the London Road.

These devices were important to the growth of the town as they allowed housing development on low-level sites where it would not otherwise have been possible.

F13   Pumping Station   ★
Woodgate Way   603457

For many years there has been a Sewage Pumping Station beside the Somerhill Stream on the south-east side of the bridge which now carries Woodgate Way over it. It is a rectangular brick building housing an electrically-powered pump. A screening device stands beside it and can sometimes be seen in operation. The Station is one of a number in the town which serve the same function as the earlier ejectors (see F12).

F14   Flood Control Barrier   ★
Between Leigh and Haysden   563460

As industry and commerce developed on the river banks and along the lower High Street, the perennial problem of flooding in the town grew worse. Floods were so frequent that many concerns developed their own ad hoc defences to keep the water out – not always very effectively. After particularly disastrous floods in 1968 the decision was taken to give the town permanent and effective flood protection. An embankment 0.8 miles in length and up to 18 feet high was built across the flood-plain at Leigh. At its centre is a concrete sluice structure with three electrically-operated radial gates which can be raised or lowered to control the flow of water. At non-flood times the river flows normally through these and down a newly-dug stretch of river, the New River Medway Channel, to rejoin its original course. At times of flood the gates

F   Utilities and services

limit the amount of water flowing through the town. Surplus water floods land upstream from the barrier, by agreement with the landowners who receive compensation, and is released as soon as circumstances allow.

The Leigh Barrier was completed in 1982 and has been used about twice a year on average. With a capacity of 7.3 million cubic yards, the floodable storage area is the largest on-line reservoir in Europe. To date it has been filled to capacity three times, most recently in October 2000.

F14

Electricity

With its gasworks well established, Tonbridge was in no hurry to embrace the electric age. But in the 1890s a number of electricity undertakings from elsewhere in the south-east began to show an interest in setting up in Tonbridge, and this prompted the Tonbridge Council to act. A Provisional Order was obtained from the Board of Trade in 1897, empowering the Council to set up its own electric lighting undertaking to serve the District. But two more years elapsed before the decision was taken to construct an 'electric light station' at the Slade, adjacent to the Hilden Brook which would serve for delivery of coal for the steam engines that would power the generators. The power station (F15) was on land which had previously been the kitchen garden of the Castle mansion, recently acquired by the Council. The consultant engineer for the project was Mr Robert Hammond, a leading campaigner for public electric lighting who 20 years earlier had set up the first continuous electricity supply in Europe, and perhaps the world, in Brighton.

In 1902, cabling was laid under the streets of Tonbridge to provide a mains supply for an area extending from the Quarry Hill/Brook Street junction, up the High Street as far as the London Road/Dry Hill Park Road junction, and including the Dry Hill area. Pavement inspection covers bearing the date 1902 survive in a few places (F16). Current began to flow on Saturday 29th November, but with only 35 street lamps then installed, and a small number of private consumers, the total demand on the first evening was just 23 kilowatts. The station supplied direct current (d.c.) at a voltage of 220 volts for lighting, and either 220 or 440 volts to run electric motors. A set of storage batteries maintained the supply at times of low demand, when it was not economical to run the steam engines.

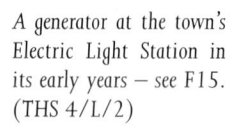

A generator at the town's Electric Light Station in its early years – see F15. (THS 4/L/2)

Except in the High Street, the street lamps were of the 'Nernst' type, in which the glowing element was a piece of ceramic material, rather than the metal filament which later became the norm. A string of 18 of the much brighter, but temperamental, Crompton arc lamps was set up to replace the gas lamps in the High Street, but teething troubles prevented their coming into service until July 1903. Five years later the Gas Company was still complaining that its gas lamps would do the job better.

By April 1904 the electricity system was serving 100 private consumers, and electric street lighting was replacing gas along the route of new mains in Pembury Road, The Drive, Bank Street, Castle Street, and Yardley Park Road. In 1905 the Council made an offer of three months' free electricity to new customers, and the system began to grow rapidly. By 1908 the first of several enlargements of the power station was necessary, as more than 7000 lamps (of 30-35 watts each) were now connected. The expanded system coped well with the temporary extra demand of more than 3000 lamps strung up to illuminate the town in celebration of the Coronation of King George V in 1911.

By the mid-20s it was clear that by setting up a d.c. system, the Council had backed the wrong horse, and conversion to alternating current (a.c.) was essential. This meant setting up a complete new system of a.c. mains alongside the existing d.c. supply. The process was not completed until the mid-30s, and for existing customers the d.c. network remained in operation until 1950.

Cast iron roadside 'distribution pillars' from this era survive in a few places in the town (e.g. F17), as do some of the switch boxes used for turning the street lighting on and off. In 1926 a Bulk Intake Station was constructed on St Stephen's Green (just north of the churchyard) where power could be brought in by underground high tension cable from Tunbridge Wells, which had adopted the a.c. system since its start in 1895 – albeit at the unorthodox frequency of 67.5 cycles/second.

One consequence of the conversion to alternating current was the appearance in

F   Utilities and services   71

the High Street of the first public electric clock, claimed to be 'absolutely accurate'. This was installed in the turret of the National Provincial Bank (now Pizza Express) overlooking the Great Bridge. The manager claimed that it was such a boon to the town that the Council should pay for its running and upkeep, which they agreed to do.

F15   Electric Light Station   ★
The Slade   588467

Tonbridge Council's Electricity Generating Station was built in 1902. It originally housed two 60kW d.c. generators powered by steam engines, and a set of storage batteries. A 150 kW steam-powered generator was added in 1909, and a 100 kW diesel-powered one in 1913. Subsequently most of Tonbridge's electricity was imported in bulk from Tunbridge Wells, and the Tonbridge station ceased generating altogether in 1951. Generating plant and other equipment were removed, and the boiler house and chimney demolished. Part of the remaining building, the Engine Room, was the home of Seeboard's 'Milne Museum' for a few years from 1975, and is now a depot for Masts, Towers and Cables Ltd. The town's main 33kV electricity intake substation remains on an adjacent site. The Milne Museum subsequently reopened as part of Amberley Museum in West Sussex.

F16   Electricity Inspection Cover   ★
Dry Hill Road/London Road   59074724

One of a number of square covers of iron and concrete dating from the original mains installation in the town and carrying the words 'Tonbridge Electricity Supply 1902'. This example is on the pavement at the junction of London Road and Dry Hill Road.

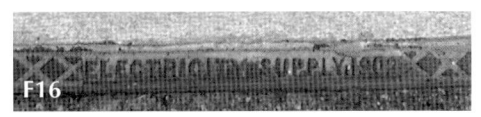

F17   Electricity pillar and   ★
switch boxes
Waterloo Road   586458

A rectangular cast iron Distribution Pillar housing cable junctions for the mains supply stands on the pavement on the west side of Waterloo Road. The smaller box on a pedestal alongside housed switchgear for the electric street lights in the area. Boxes of this type were installed in the 1920s and 30s, and a number remain, still apparently in use, in various parts of the town.

F18   Electric Street   ★
Lamp
Bourne Lane   595471

One of a number of cast iron lamp posts still to be found in the town bearing the manufacturer's name of Seale, Austen and Barnes (see D4). Bourne Lane, on land adjoining Hadlow Road that was previously part of Bourne Farm, was given its name in 1923, and the lamps installed the following year.

F19   Private generating station   ★
Somerhill estate   609453

A building adjacent to the old Somerhill gas works (F3) once housed Somerhill's electricity generating plant, said to have been powered by a paraffin engine. Somerhill was connected to the public mains supply, with its own transformer, in 1938.

The Fire Service

Organised fire-fighting in Tonbridge appears to have begun with George Hooper, a lawyer, who donated leather fire buckets for communal use. On his death in 1744 he left forty pounds for 'a water engine or engines to be placed in the parish church' (F20). In 1747 fire-fighting was the responsibility of the Lighting and Watching Committee of the Parish Vestry – the body of male ratepayers which ran the town at that time. The equipment was later stored in a barn in Church Street (now called 'Fire-cart Barn') and then at the Crown Yard, behind the Local Board offices at 83 High Street (now the site of Barclay's Bank). By 1870 the brigade consisted of a Superintendent and nine volunteer firemen, and was under the auspices of the Lighting Committee of the Local Board. From 1889 the volunteers were summoned by a steam horn at the Water Works. A new fire station opened in Bank Street in 1902 (F24) and housed a Salamander steam pump, initially horse-drawn. The Fire Service transferred from local to county control in 1948, and the station moved to its present premises in Vale Road in 1985.

F20 Fire hooks ★
In the porch of the Parish Church 591467

From 1747, tools for fire-fighting were kept in the Parish Church, and two long-handled fire hooks remain there, on either side of the entrance, inside the porch. They were used to pull the thatch off burning roofs or drag out items of property from blazing buildings. One originally had a ring for harnessing a horse to do the pulling, but this had to be cut off to fit the hooks into their present position. According to Neve they were last used at a blaze involving haystacks and farm buildings in the Slade in 1876.

F21 Fire Insurance marks ★
1 & 2 Church Street 591466

Fire-marks were displayed on properties to show which premises carried fire insurance, and also to advertise the insurance companies. A fire-mark for the Nottingham and Derbyshire Fire and Life Assurance Company is displayed on the front of No. 1 Church Street, and one for the Norwich Union Fire Insurance Company next door at No. 2. Both are believed to be originals. The nearby Rose & Crown inn also carried fire-marks, and two of these have been preserved and are displayed in the hotel's restaurant.

F22 Hydrant cover ★
South end of Church Street 59194663

In 1890 it was recommended that ten new fire hydrants be installed in the town, and this plate, in Church Street, may cover one of them. The lettering TLB stands for Tonbridge Local Board which was the responsible authority at the time. Similar covers for hydrant points providing water for fire-fighting are found throughout the town. Some are marked TLB, others TUDC (Tonbridge Urban District Council, from 1894), TFB (Tonbridge Fire Brigade, after 1901), TWWC (Tonbridge Water Works Company), or simply FH (Fire Hydrant).

F22

F23 Indicator for Fire Hydrant ★
52 Woodside Road 585453

A 1707 Act of Parliament obliged towns to set up signs indicating the location of hydrants for fire-fighting. The signs may include the distance in feet and inches of the hydrant from

F   Utilities and services

the service indicator. Diamond-shaped plates of white enamel remain on walls in a few places in the town. This one is at 52 Woodside Road. More recent indicators have square yellow plates on a concrete roadside post.

F24   Former Fire Station   ★
Bank Street   590466

The new Fire Station which opened in 1902 bears a memorial plaque and the badge of the town, and had room for two appliances. It was originally manned by one professional firefighter and 20 volunteers. The horse-drawn 'Salamander' steam pump was eventually replaced by motorised ones. The Fire Station served until 1985, when a new one opened in Vale Road, but the building remains in use as offices and meeting space.

G   Communications and entertainment

The Postal Service

Organised public postal services between larger towns began to be established in the seventeenth century. Tonbridge had its own post office in 1672, with a daily service to and from London by postboys on horseback. An overnight postal service to London was made possible by the improvement in roads and the coming of regular stagecoach services. In 1839 the 'Royal Mail' coach reached the Rose and Crown from Hastings at 1.30 every morning and went on to London, while the reverse service arrived in Tonbridge at midnight.

Thirty years later, with mail carried by train, there were three deliveries to and from London daily. Within the town, postmen set off on delivery rounds at 7 a.m. (7.30 in winter), 12 noon, and 3.15 p.m..

In 1848 William Ware was the Tonbridge postmaster and the Post Office was on his premises at 101 and 103 High Street, now Nos. 129 (Lambeth Building Society) and 131 (Ward and Partners). Chapman records that letters were posted through a slot in a wooden board which replaced part of the window glass. A (recent) pillar box still stands on the pavement at this point. From 1896 to 1915 the Post Office occupied new premises at 91 High Street (now Pizza Express) before moving down to the new General Post Office, Sorting Office and Telephone Exchange at 94 High Street (G2).

The General Post Office in c.1920 – see G2. Hall's Garage, adjoining, was demolished in the 1930s. (THS 14A/430)

G Communications and entertainment

G1 Victorian Post Box ★
Railway Station 587460

The wall-mounted box on Platform 2 at Tonbridge Railway station is believed to be the only letter box remaining in the town from Queen Victoria's reign (1837-1901). A wall box dating from Edward VII's reign (1901-10) can be seen outside Whitworth House at the junction of Dry Hill Road and Dry Hill Park Crescent, and there is a fine George V (1910-36) pillar box outside Boots in the High Street.

G2 Old Post Office ★
94 High Street 590464

Tonbridge's new four-storey General Post Office opened in 1915 at 94 High Street, former site of the Loggerheads public house (A20). It also housed the Sorting Office (behind) and, until 1939, the Telephone Exchange, on the first floor, where calls were still connected manually, and in 1923 there was still no night operator. It remained in use as the Post Office until the 1990s when it became vacant following the opening of the new area sorting office in Vale Rise in 1983 and the removal of the Post Office counter to Angel Walk. The building is now Wetherspoon's 'Humphrey Bean' pub. The words 'Post Office' and a George V cipher remain above the entrance.

Telegraph and telephone

The age of electric communication reached Tonbridge in the 1840s, when the South-Eastern Railway laid telegraph wires alongside all its lines, including the London to Dover main line through Tonbridge. The driving force behind this enterprise was the South-Eastern's eminent telegraph engineer, Mr Charles V. Walker, who was a resident of the town for a few years in the 1840s and 50s. At one time he even kept a telegraph instrument in his home on the 'Hastings Road', linked in to the railway system by wire, for the personal use of himself and his wife. The location of this 'Superintendent's House' has not yet been identified.

Tonbridge was the nerve-centre of the South-Eastern's telegraph network, which included forty-seven linked telegraph offices by 1850. The busy Tonbridge office (G3) was in the original railway station in Priory Road.

A side-effect of the coming of the telegraph was the availability for the first time of precisely-known time in the town. From 1852 a time-signal direct from the Royal Observatory was received at the telegraph office daily, and the railway company was at liberty to pass this 'Greenwich time' to local clock and watch makers.

Tonbridge Telegraph Office (see G3) from C.V. Walker's book 'Electric Telegraph Manipulation', 1850. An operator uses one of the instruments (right), while the supervisor sits at his desk.

After the station moved to its new site, the telegraph office was on the road bridge, across the road from the present station entrance, on the top floor of a building that was destroyed by fire in 1916 or 1917. Telegraph services were nationalised under the Post Office in 1870, and an 1886 Town Directory mentions a telegraph office at the main Post Office in the High Street, where telegrams could be sent at a new reduced rate of sixpence for 12 words. By 1894-5 there were also telegraph offices at rural Post Offices in Five Oak Green, Hadlow, Hildenborough, Leigh, Marden, Paddock Wood, Penshurst, and Shipbourne. Forty people are listed as telegraph office employees in Tonbridge in the 1881 census. By 1920 the telegraph was past its heyday, overtaken by the growing telephone network, though its lingering death took another fifty years.

The telephone had started in America in 1876, when Alexander Graham Bell took out a patent. By the end of the following year the enterprising Mr Walker (by now a Fellow of the Royal Society) had set up his own experimental telephone line, using a surplus telegraph cable, between Tonbridge and Redhill. In 1878 this pioneering experiment was extended to London, and both speech and song were successfully communicated between Tonbridge and the capital.

Ten years later, the South of England Telephone Company opened its exchange in Tunbridge Wells and began to canvass for subscribers. Tonbridge was connected by a line through the Somerhill Estate, but there were only two subscribers in the town in the early 1890s. Expansion began after the National Telephone Company took over, and by 1898 there were 21 subscribers in the town. By then a Public Call Office, for use by non-subscribers, was operating at 76 High Street (and the exchange may have been there also). By 1901 the exchange and Call Office were at 15 East Street, moving again in about 1907 to 26 (now 28) Avebury Avenue, by which time there were some 140 subscribers. The National Telephone Company also had premises at 127 High Street (until recently John Hewett, Estate Agent) from about 1905-11. A minor diversion at the turn of the century was the setting up of a rival telephone network run by Tunbridge Wells Council. A few lines of this Municipal System were set up in Tonbridge in 1900-01, but by the end of 1902 the new venture had collapsed after a price war.

The National Telephone Company was taken over by the Post Office in 1912, though its name is still visible on one pavement Pit Cover in the town (see G4). Three years later the grand new Post Office and Telephone Exchange opened in the High Street (G2). All calls were connected manually, and in 1923 there was still no night operator, although the resident caretaker could be called on to make connections if necessary. The new purpose-built telephone exchange in Avebury Avenue (G7) bears the date 1939, and is still in use, though much expanded. In 1931 the Post Office applied to the Council for permission to set up public telephone kiosks at various points in the town. A few red phone boxes still remain, of which at least one probably dates from the 1930s (G6).

G Communications and entertainment

G3 Telegraph Office ●
First railway Station 589460

The first Tonbridge telegraph office was in the original railway station in Priory Road (see H27), and opened in 1845 or 6 when Charles Walker and William Cooke installed the electric telegraph along all the lines of the South-Eastern Railway. In addition to carrying the traffic necessary for running the trains, it served the needs of private users. Telegrams – messages for transmission as electrical pulses letter by letter – could be handed in there, and replies received. The charge was initially very high, five shillings for a reply-paid twenty-word message (equivalent to nearly £10 today), but was subsequently reduced. After the station moved to its new site, the telegraph office was on the road bridge, across the road from the present station entrance, on the top floor of a building that was destroyed by fire in 1916 or 1917. After nationalisation of the telegraph system in 1870 there was also an office in the Post Office.

G4 Footway Box cover ★
Springwell Road/Quarry Hill 58554556

Rectangular Footway boxes giving access to underground cables, are found on pavements throughout the town at intervals of a few hundred yards. They can be roughly dated by the wording on the reinforced concrete cover. This one, on the south side of Springwell Road, is the only survivor from the era of the National Telephone Company, whose origins date from efforts to exploit Alexander Graham Bell's telephone patents in Britain in 1878. National was taken over by the General Post Office in 1912. Covers with the words 'Post Office Telegraphs', e.g. outside No. 9 London Road, were in use from 1905 to the 1940s, when the wording changed to 'Post Office Telephones'. Later covers are labelled 'GPO' from the 1960s and 'BT' or 'Telecom' from the 1970s. Covers with the letters 'CATV' are common on pavements throughout the town and give access to the optical fibre cables laid in the late 1990s for Cable TV.

G5 G.P.O. Service Indicator ★
East Street 59164661

Kerbside posts mark the position of cable junction access points under the roadway. This early example, outside No. 16 East Street, is the only survivor in the town from George V's reign (1910-36). It would originally have indicated the distance from the post to the junction access point.

G6 Telephone Box ★
High Street, outside Ferox Hall 591470

This box is of the K6 type designed by the architect Sir Giles Gilbert Scott to commemorate the silver jubilee of King George V and Queen Mary in 1935. 'Jubilee' K6s were the first national standard telephone kiosk and continued to be made until the 1960s. This one bears the cipher of King George VI (1936-52) and was probably installed in the late 1930s. It was made by the Lion Foundry of Kirkintilloch and like many of its type it is a listed building.

Earlier phone boxes were near the Big Bridge, at the Pinnacles, and by Lovers' Walk in Hadlow Road. These were approved by the Council in 1931, but the original boxes do not survive.

G7 Telephone Exchange ★
Avebury Avenue 587462

Tonbridge's 1939 telephone exchange, adjacent to 28 Avebury Avenue, is typical of many of its era. It replaced an earlier exchange in the main Post Office (G2). It is marked as 'Automatic Telephone Exchange' on a 1962 map, indicating that by then subscribers could dial their local calls. Much expanded, it remains in use.

Cinemas and other places of recreation

Entertainments have grown almost continually in the last few hundred years. Especially during the last century their number and variety have surged, encouraged by more leisure and rising incomes among the mass of the population. The physical structures and sites for recreation were largely created in the last 100 or 150 years.

As is well-known, playgoing was popular from the Tudor period, with suitable buildings developing first in London and then in provincial towns. Theatres and music halls became widespread in the later nineteenth century. The great new medium of mass entertainment in the twentieth century was the cinema. It took women with their husbands from their homes to enjoy themselves for the first time; a big proportion of the population went once or twice a week. Like many medium-sized towns Tonbridge between the 1910s and 1970s had up to three or four cinemas showing films at the same time (G8-G13), and a theatre (G14) and skating rink (G15) for parts of the period. Only with the general spread of television by the 1960s and 1970s have cinemas gradually been closed as entertainment reverted to the home.

Turning to sport, horse-racing and unorganized and organized football and cricket are many hundred years old. Racing was the first to create permanent courses and viewing stands, by the eighteenth century. Boosted by the huge growth of the suburban middle classes, who supplied the leadership, and the rising interest of artisans and workers, who provided the bulk of the watchers, cricket, soccer and rugby clubs, the first two with professional players, were set up widely in the later 19th century. In addition to extensive grounds, these sports have needed pavilions for changing clothes and perhaps the provision of refreshments and seats. Lawn tennis began in the later 1870s and golf, originating from Scotland, developed in the 1880s, both involving women as well as men.

In Tonbridge cricket has been played at least since the early nineteenth century, certainly behind Tonbridge School and probably on the Racecourse sports ground,

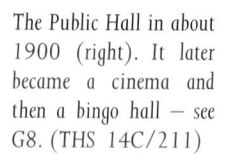

The Public Hall in about 1900 (right). It later became a cinema and then a bingo hall – see G8. (THS 14C/211)

G   Communications and entertainment

with the Angel Ground (G16) being first used in the 1890s. Until 1939 the Kent County Cricket Club played two matches on the Angel Ground in June. The Club Nursery was in Tonbridge between the 1890s and 1920s. There have been several golf courses, lawn tennis courts and a swimming pool since 1910, with the river available for boating and swimming. In the twentieth century the Sports Ground (G17) has been used for soccer, rugby, and hockey as well as tennis and bowls.

Horse riding and traction for pleasure were fundamental until near the end of the 19th century. Then cheap bicycles and the much dearer motor cars and lorries became available. Ice skating on frozen ponds is an age-old sport; indoor skating rinks emerged before the First World War. Where rivers and lakes have been present boating, sailing and especially swimming have been enjoyed since the 19th century (see C24), with swimming baths being built almost everywhere, with one at least in each town.

G8   Capitol Cinema

176 High Street   590468

This was built largely in brick in about 1876 to be the Public Hall. It was opened as the Capitol Cinema by J. H. Taylor in 1921, unchanged externally, but with a new entrance, crush hall, tearoom, 250-seat balcony, armchair seating, and high narrow screen inside. The cinema was out of use due to fire from December 1926 to October 1928, when an organ was put in. It was managed by the Tonbridge Cinemas Co. from 1933-39, Kent and Associated Cinemas from 1939-56, and Shipman and King from 1956-64, after which it became a bingo hall. This was damaged by fire in an adjacent property in 1997 and demolished in 2004-5.

The Capitol Cinema in 1931 (THS 5/233)

G9   Central Picture Hall

62 High Street   589463

This cinema was open from 1910-14 in a former chapel and public hall, after some alteration. The building was a furniture store from 1914-35. The B-wise store now stands on the site.

G10   Star Cinema

Bradford Street   589463

The Star Cinema occupied the former fellmonger's warehouse in Bradford Street. It was opened in 1910 by Charles Wilson of the Bull Hotel, who also began other cinemas, and held 600 people. Augustus Johnson took over in 1911, but the cinema closed in 1914. It was opened again from 1930-39. The 1952 Crown Building now occupies the site.

G11   Empire Picture Palace

10 and 12 Avebury Avenue   588461

The Empire was run from 1914-32 by 'Buster' West who also ran other cinemas in Tonbridge, Horsham, Guildford and elsewhere. From 1932-55 it served as a playhouse (theatre). The site on the corner of River Lawn Road now forms part of a Health Club.

G12   Pavilion Cinema

Avebury Avenue   588461

The Pavilion was run by 'Buster' West and others from 1921-41, with seating for 656 people. The site is now part of the County Library.

G13   Ritz Cinema

Botany   590463

The Ritz was Tonbridge's largest cinema, with its own café, wide staircase and balcony. It was opened by Union Cinemas in 1937 and closed in 1978 by Shipman and King, its managers since 1955. It then ran as a 98-seat minicinema until 1981. The building remained until 2001, when it was demolished as part of the Waitrose development.

G14 Medway Hall •
New Wharf Road/Bradford Street   589464

This was a large wooden structure, opened in 1922 for meetings, shows and dances. It was demolished in c.1970 and the site is now the car park for Somerfield.

G15 Empire Skating Rink •
Bradford Street   589463

The rink opened for roller skating in 1918 in a large single-storey wooden structure, known in the 1920s and 30s as the Empire Skating Rink, and was popular with younger people. It closed in 1939 and probably did not reopen, as by 1950 it was in use as the 'Empire Hall' for furniture dealing. It was ruined in the 1968 flooding and the site is now the lower portion of the Bradford Street car park.

The Skating Rink in c.1912 (THS 5/219)

G16 The Angel Ground •
Angel Centre and adjacent car parks   590462

The 10-acre site was bought by Tonbridge Cricket Club in 1905 for £4300, helped by a public subscription of £2000. From 1897-1927 it was also the seat of the Kent County C.C. Nursery, managed first by Tom Pawley. Until 1939 the cricket included Kent cricket week, with two county matches, in June. The ground was also used for athletics, military tattoos etc. until it was destroyed by the army in the Second World War. It was bought by the U. D. C. in 1947 and let to the Tonbridge Football Club, members of the Southern League, for nearly 28 years. It had a pavilion, a covered stand for 2000, and a total capacity up to about 7000. In the late 1970s a great leisure centre with a big car park was planned, the complex being opened in 1982. A reminder of the presence of the Angel Ground remains in the form of cast-iron balconies on the side of 43 High Street, adjacent to the Little Bridge, which would originally have afforded a fine view over the Ground.

G17 The Racecourse Sportsground ★
West of the town   585465

The Sportsground (also known as the Racecourse) is an area of some 50 acres, bounded by the Medway and its tributaries. In the 18th century this area, in the flood plain, was part of the Castle Estate. It was taken over by the Water Works Company in the 1850s. The land was leased as pasture to local farmers, who also established the unofficial racetrack along the north side. Racing took place on two days in August 1871, according to reports in the *Tonbridge Free Press*, and continued until the early 1900s when it was banned because of rowdyism. An early race card is reproduced below.

After the Angel Ground was built in 1905, the Invicta Harriers used the Sportsground. By 1910, and probably years earlier, football and cricket were being played there. The Urban District Council bought it in 1923 with a loan of £4080. There were reported to be 7 football and a hockey pitch in 1922 and 57 tennis courts, 12 cricket pitches, a miniature golf course and a quoit pitch, run with the help of the Sports Association, in 1923. The Ground held various small pavilions and huts built of wood for the various sports. A metal plaque on the footbridge linking the Sportsground to Avebury Avenue commemorates the official opening of the bridge and sports ground in 1923.

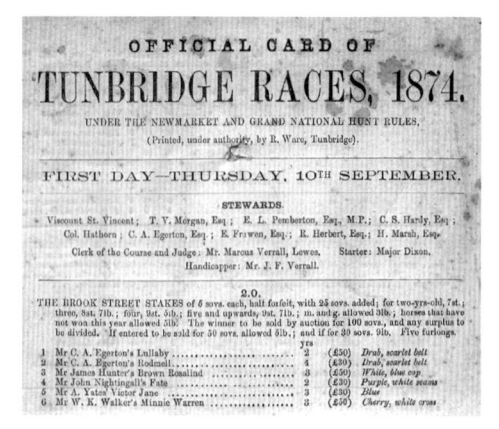

Part of an Official Card for Tonbridge Racecourse, printed by R. Ware in 1874, showing runners in the 'Brook Street Stakes' – see G17. (THS archives)

H Transport

Roads and bridges

An iron age track (H1) ran north-south across the river where Tonbridge now stands and has defined the axis of the town ever since. After the Norman conquest the Tonbridge crossing also became part of an important route from London to Normandy via Rye and other ports. The road from London met what is now Shipbourne Road at a T-junction opposite the Star and Garter, but was later re-routed on the present curved track into the High Street. At the south end of the town travellers could either take the Frant Road which curved to the right along part of Barden Road and then Waterloo Road before climbing Quarry Hill, or the Rye and Hastings route which started along what is now Vale Road before climbing up to Primrose Hill, now the upper part of Pembury Road. Both these routes were later disrupted by the railway.

In the 1580s a strip of the High Street six yards wide from Church Lane down to the Market Cross (East Street) was paved with stones, but most roads in and around the town remained in a deplorable state. More of the High Street was paved with broken stone in the 1750s and 'macadamisation' began in the town in the 1820s. This produced a much smoother cambered surface by the use of smaller stones bound together with earth and sand, and compacted by the passage of wheeled traffic. Many roads in the town were tar-sprayed in 1910, by which time motor vehicles were beginning to make their presence felt.

Outside the town, the first improvements came with the 'turnpiking' of main routes, which involved Acts of Parliament to set up Trusts empowered to charge tolls and use the income to improve and maintain the main roads. The route from Sevenoaks to Woodsgate via Tonbridge, with a spur from Pembury to Tunbridge Wells, was turnpiked in 1709. It was originally 16 miles long, with 10 tollgates, 3 of them sited in Tonbridge. Other turnpikes followed, from Maidstone to Tunbridge Wells via Tonbridge in 1765, and from Ightham to Tonbridge in 1809. Most turnpikes remained in operation until about 1870, by which time the railways had stolen much of the traffic. Journeys to Tunbridge Wells were eased by the cutting of a new macadamised road through Quarry Hill in 1808. Better roads brought faster travel so that in 1836 the Royal Mail stagecoach that left

Looking north-east up Hadlow Road, at the junction with Mill Lane. The tollgate was removed in 1868 and the keeper's house demolished. Tollgate House, in the background, remains. (THS 15/HR2)

London for Hastings at 7.30 pm came through Tonbridge before midnight.

The disruption caused by the railway resulted in new road-building in the south of the town in the 1840s. The new straight road that now passes the railway station carried the rerouted Tunbridge Wells traffic, while Pembury Road was built for the Hastings road.

The High Street was widened by demolishing all properties on the west side and building new, starting from the south end in the 1890s and working up to the Big Bridge some 40 years later. The purpose was to ease traffic congestion, and the width was increased from less than 30 ft to over 50 ft. The High Street was also the A21, and remained the only north-south through route in the town right up to 1971 when the western bypass opened. The 'mini-bypass' linking Cannon Lane and Vale Road on the eastern side had opened the previous year. Other road improvements include Cornwallis Avenue in 1930, bypassing the tortuous route to Hadlow and Maidstone through Hadlow Stair, and the Woodgate link from Vale Road to the A21 in the 1990s. Vestiges of earlier roadways remain in various places, principally in Somerhill Park (H2), at the top of Quarry Hill, and Old Hadlow Road. The short service road outside Nos. 1-6 Shipbourne Road shows how Dry Hill (as it once was) ran before it was replaced by the present regraded roadway alongside, while the raised pavement in Waterloo Road indicates how the Tunbridge Wells road once ran. A brick-paved area remains outside Mill Cottage at the bottom of Mill Lane, and some old paving has been preserved at the east end of Church Lane.

The High Street, looking north, c. 1907. The street in the foreground has been widened, while the rest remains to be done. The white building is Seale, Austen and Barnes, ironmongers (D4), adjacent to New Wharf Road. (THS 14A/117)

H1   Roman trackway   ★

Shipbourne Road / Rowan Shaw   596490

The Romans built no new roads in the Tonbridge area, but would have maintained, and upgraded, the pre-existing north-south trackway through the town. This served for transporting iron from the Weald up to North Kent. Margary in the mid-20th century traced its route from Cross-in-Hand in Sussex, through Frant, Southborough, Tonbridge and Shipbourne to Wrotham.

In north Tonbridge it ran parallel to, and a few yards to the east of, Shipbourne Road between Yardley Park Road and the Pen Stream bridge. A low bank (the 'agger'), crowned with a wooden fence, now marks its course along the wooded verge between Rowan Shaw and Shipbourne Road. Excavation here in the

H Transport

1980s found the ancient track, some 4 yards wide and metalled with ironstone and flint fragments, lying 5-10 inches below the present surface. An earlier dig on the same line in the Cage Green area found a surface whose metalling of sandstone and iron slag had rusted into a solid surface.

H2   Old Rye road   ★
Somerhill Park   597449

After turnpiking, the road to Rye and Hastings left Tonbridge along a substantial causeway that now forms the sliproad onto the southbound A21, running along the boundary of Somerhill Park. In earlier days the road ran inside the park at its eastern extremity, crossing the Somerhill Stream on a stone bridge and rejoining the present route part way up Castle Hill. Part of this old road remains and is accessible as a public footpath, starting by the North Lodge near the junction of Woodgate Way and Pembury Road.

H2

H3   The Great Bridge   ★
High Street   590464

Tonbridge is an historic crossing point on the Medway plain, where a bridge of some description has existed since 1191. In 1525 Henry VIII, as lord of Tonbridge Castle, had a narrow five-arched sandstone bridge built. This was replaced in 1775-6 by a new Great Bridge, with three arches and a stone parapet, designed and built for £1100 by Robert Mylne who had earlier been responsible for Blackfriars Bridge in London. A form of iron railing was introduced in 1818. The present bridge, often known as the Big Bridge, was designed to minimise obstruction to the flow of water. It opened in 1888 and was widened in the 1920s in line with the wider High Street.

H4   The Lower Bridge   ★
High Street   589463

There were once five stone bridges at intervals along the High Street crossing five branches of the river. Now only the Great Bridge and Lower Bridge remain, the other streams between them having been filled in or culverted when the High Street was widened. The Lower, or Little, Bridge spans what was once the main stream of the Medway, and had two arches. It was rebuilt after being swept away by floods and ice in 1814, and again in 1872.

H5   Sutton's Bridge   ●
High Street   589463

A stone on the north-facing wall of No. 53 High Street marked the former location of Sutton's Bridge, which carried the High Street over one of the lesser Medway streams at this point. The stone commemorated the repair of the bridge by the County in 1628, and was due to be replaced by a replica in 2005 after the original was damaged.

The three-arched Big Bridge in 1796, with barges at the Town Wharf, engraved from a painting by Paul Sandby. (THS 16/13)

H6   Cannon Lane bridge   ★
Cannon Lane   596465

The present Medway bridge in Cannon Lane, barely noticed by motorists on the mini-bypass, opened in 1970 when the new link road was completed. It replaced a narrower steel girder bridge.

There was no crossing here before 1677, when provision was made for a road and bridges to link Postern Forge and the Town Mill. Part of the route of this road remains as the curved lay-by outside Darby's. The Cannon Lane bridge caused trouble after the Medway Navigation opened in 1741 because it was too low, and was raised several times before collapsing in 1811, to be replaced by a new one. This, though higher, still caused some barges to get stuck, to be released only by lowering the water level.

H7   Medway Viaduct (A21)   ★
Western side of the town   561461

After decades of discussion, and the Ministry's rejection of an eastern route to relieve traffic on the industrial side of town, the A21 Tonbridge bypass was opened by the then Prime Minister, Edward Heath, on 12th July 1971, as a continuation of the Sevenoaks bypass built three years earlier. Its 6.5 mile length was built across local terrain 'of a particularly unpredictable nature', according to the contractor, at a cost of more than £5 million. It includes the 1500 ft 15-span Medway viaduct, mainly of precast concrete, carrying the two carriageways over the river, the railway and the flood barrier. Further major works were needed to create a two-level intersection at the top of Quarry Hill.

Street Furniture

A number of historic pieces of street furniture survive in the town and are listed here. Others can be found in sections F (Utilities and services) and G (Communications and entertainment).

H8   Mileplate   ★
Quarry Hill/Pembury Road   58714588

An iron plate mounted in the wall of No. 8 Quarry Hill Parade, north of the junction with Pembury Road, bears the inscription 'London 31 / Tonbridge 1'. It was originally sited at the top of Lavender Hill/Pembury Road.

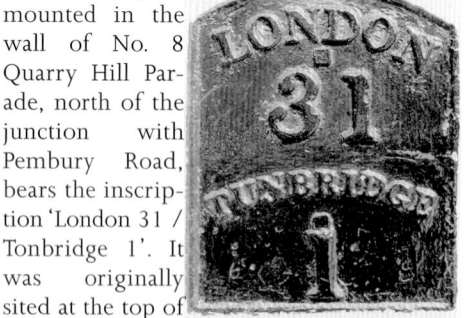

Stone mileposts now lacking their plates can still be seen in London Road, facing Smythe House (58944728), and in the layby where the southbound slip road merges into the A21 on Castle Hill (59984475).

H9   Tollgate marker   ★
High Street/Avebury Avenue   58844613

An iron post stands outside the Public Library, facing down Vale Road, to mark the former location of a tollgate. It was put up by the the Urban District Council but is undated. Identical tollgate markers are sited behind railings in Shipbourne Road, opposite the Filling Station (5919 4758), and in Hadlow Road, against the curved wall at the Mill Lane junction (59414682).

H10   Drinking Trough   ★
High Street/Bank Street   59054661

A granite trough stands on the pavement on the west side of the High Street outside the National Westminster Bank at the corner of

Bank Street. It is inscribed 'Metropolitan Drinking Fountain and Cattle Trough Association'. There is no date on it but it must have been brought here after 1913 because there was another trough nearby until this date. The Metropolitan Drinking Fountain and Cattle Trough Association installed more than 1000 troughs in London and elsewhere, starting in 1859. The charity still exists.

H11 Drinking Trough ★
Quarry Hill/Waterloo Road 58594569

A granite trough stands in Quarry Hill at the end of St Stephen's churchyard at the junction with Waterloo Road. It bears on one side the words 'Drink, let the cattle drink also' and on the other 'This trough originally stood in the High Street on / the site of the ancient Market Place Market House / the stocks and whipping post / owing to the increase of traffic it was removed to this spot in 1913'. At one end of the trough is a drinking fountain with the words 'The Gift of Mrs George Wise / Tunbridge 1902'.

H12 Drinking Fountain ★
Quarry Hill/Waterloo Road 58594569

This fountain was constructed in 1857 at the end of St Stephen's churchyard at the junction of Quarry Hill and Waterloo Road. It is made of stone in an octagonal shape with a pointed roof; there is a step for children to use. The worn inscription round the edge of the roof is 'That the Weary may Rest'. According to Chapman it was erected in the hope that the chain horse men waiting to haul loads up Quarry Hill would slake their thirst there rather than visit the Imperial pub nearby. A similar fountain erected outside the Star and Garter at the junction of London and Shipbourne Roads in 1872 has gone.

H13 Roadside Shelter ★
Quarry Hill/Pembury Road junction 586 458

The shelter backs onto St Stephen's churchyard and is obscured by the roundabout. It has a tiled roof and two long wooden seats. A metal plate on the wall is inscribed 'For the aged and weary. This shelter was provided by the Town Wardens. T. Ives. H.J.M. Watts JP. 1930'. The Town Wardens are the Trustees of a long-standing local charity.

H14 Boundary Post ★
London Road/Portman Park 59144708

This iron post backs onto the boundary wall of Tonbridge School near the traffic lights opposite Portman Park. It is similar to others within the school grounds and was erected when the governors bought land for the main cricket field in 1829, to mark the limits of school property. It is 2ft 6 in high and bears the coat of arms of the Skinners' Company (the school governors), the date 1826, and a geometrical design with a diamond shape and crosses.

H15 Boundary Post ★
Brightfriars 58294675

An iron post, 60 cm (2 ft) high, stands on Brightfriars (now part of the Racecourse sports ground) and bears the letters 'TW' for Town Wardens, and '1904'. It marks a boundary of one of the 'town lands'– parcels of land formerly held by the Town Wardens, income from which was used for upkeep of the town's bridges and roads.

The post is beside the footpath which follows a stream from the Slade to

Hayesden, at the point where it meets another path coming at right angles from a concrete bridge over the northern branch of the Medway. Two further posts stand alongside this second path. The set of posts defines the straightening in 1904 of a former irregular boundary.

H16   Boundary post   ★
Bank Street   59044673

This iron post bears the letters 'TMC' which refer to the Tonbridge Stock and Cattle Market Company formed in 1855. It stands against a corner of No. 3 Bank Street and marks a boundary of the market site. It also carries the maker's name 'Seale, Tonbridge'.

H17   Coal hole cover   ★
High Street   59074654

A coal hole cover has been preserved in the pavement outside No. 91 High Street (Pizza Express). The 15-inch diameter plate bears the name of Hayward Brothers of Union Street, Borough, in south-east London, a large-scale supplier of coal hole covers in the mid to late 19th century. The plate could be removed to allow delivery of coal directly into the cellar of the adjacent building.

H18   Bench mark   ★
Lambert's Yard   58914625

Bench marks were used as reference points by the surveyors of the Ordnance Survey before the GPS satellite system took over. Bench marks were mainly cut in the period 1912-21 and although the O. S. no longer supports the Bench mark system, a number of marks remain on walls in the town. The centre of the horizontal bar indicates a precisely surveyed altitude whose value is given on large-scale maps. The mark shown here is in the wall of No. 38 High Street and marks an altitude of 76.37 feet above mean sea level at Newlyn, the chosen reference level. Other bench marks can be seen on the walls of No. 10 Bordyke and the former Methodist Church in East Street.

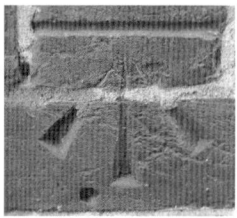

The River

No doubt in mediaeval times, and earlier, sections of the Medway were used for personal travel. Freight transport would only be in shallow craft and when river conditions allowed. Three separate initiatives to canalise the Upper Medway were launched in the 17th century, one of them with the support of the King, Charles II, who saw the river's potential for transporting cannon and timber from the Weald to the Royal Dockyards at Chatham. But none of these schemes came to fruition.

In 1740 parliament passed an Act for making the River Medway navigable from Maidstone to Forest Row in Sussex. A Medway Navigation Company was set up to raise capital, with many local shareholders, and a surveyor was appointed.

Work on the river between Maidstone and Tonbridge involved clearing existing weirs and sluices, scouring the river bed, widening and deepening it where necessary, shoring the banks, constructing locks, fords and wharves at Tonbridge (H19) and Branbridges, together with work on a number of bridges. All this was done by navvies with spades, aided by a single pumping engine. Stone from the

H   Transport

Castle was sold by its owner, John Hooker, for use in constructing some of the nearer locks.

Parts of the Navigation were ready for use by small loads as early as 1741, but it was several years before full loads could be carried all the way. Freight carried upstream in 1745 included coal, salt and lime, while timber, iron, hops and hoops, for barrels, went the other way. Later cargoes also included chalk, stone, gravel and Baltic timber on the upstream leg, while corn, wool, leather and other agricultural produce was taken back down, as for a time was gunpowder from the Leigh mills. The Navigation had no proper towpath, and barges were towed downstream by two men who took about ten hours to go from Tonbridge to Maidstone. The return journey, with three men, took longer. Sailing barges were also used.

Barges at Medway Wharf, looking downstream, with Maylam's Wharf behind – date unknown. (THS 16/16)

In 1743 the Navigation Company began to trade as a coal merchant, and later also sold timber, stone, lime and other commodities brought upriver in its own fleet of barges. Business was brisk and the town grew as a commercial centre. In 1828 the Company's prosperity attracted the attention of James Christie, described as 'an adventurer from Surrey'. He formed the Penshurst Canal Company to extend the navigable river to Penshurst, and possibly further in due course. Work was begun, but by 1832 Christie was bankrupt and had absconded to North America. Parts of the Penshurst Canal remain, finished (H22-H23) and unfinished (H24).

The Medway Company at first saw the railway as an ally, useful for distributing its coal to depots at local stations. Plans were drawn up for a canal, and then a tramway, between Medway Wharf and the railway goods yard. But the railway company did not co-operate and it soon became clear that the railway was a competitor. Although the Navigation lowered its charges and invested in a steam tug, it could not compete. A slow decline ensued until in 1910 the river became impassable and the Company collapsed. Responsibility was taken over by the Medway Board of Conservators who borrowed money to revive the Navigation which reopened in 1915. To alleviate the flood problem, the rebuilt locks were accompanied by weirs and sluices to carry the excess water. But freight traffic never revived, and in recent years only pleasure craft have been seen on the Upper Medway. Ten locks now provide a total fall of 57 feet between Tonbridge and the tidal river at Allington. Effective flood relief only came with the opening of the Leigh barrier in 1982 (F14).

H19 Medway Wharf ★
Medway Wharf Road 590464

The Medway Wharf ran for some 100 yards downstream from the Big Bridge on the south bank of the river, and Medway Wharf Road was built to serve it. The whole area was a scene of great activity where freight was transferred from cart to barge and vice versa. Early maps show a crane, weighing station, coal pens, a lime kiln (where chalk was converted to lime for mortar), and a public house, the forerunner of the existing Castle Inn. Surviving buildings include the warehouse of T. Maylam and Co., Agricultural Merchants, which has been incorporated into the Maylam's Quay building in Medway Wharf Road, and Lyons Warehouse on the opposite bank. This was used by Humphrey Wightwick, tallow chandler, and later by Charlton, the miller, and became the Hogshead pub. A single-storey building on the corner of Medway Wharf Road and the High Street, built in the mid-19th century for the Medway Company's offices and boardroom and later used by Maylam's, was demolished in 2005. The Baltic Saw Mills company had premises on the Botany side of Medway Wharf Road and more recently between Lyons Crescent and the river.

Other wharfage was available in the town, for example on the south side of the river upstream from the Big Bridge, and on the New Cut (see H22) where the planned New Wharf later became Doust's boatyard, then the Riverside Café, and finally in the 1970s an office block.

Water level in the town basin was and is

Lyons Wharf on the north bank of the river, in use as Humphrey Wightwick's warehouse. It later became the Hogshead pub. (Ton. Ref. Lib.)

controlled by the Town Lock and weir, which have been enlarged and rebuilt over the years, most recently in the 1980s. In the past this level would fall, sometimes drastically, when the owner of the Town Mill drew large amounts of water to operate the wheels.

H20 Child's lock ★
0.3 miles downstream from Cannon bridge 602467

On the original Medway Navigation the first lock downstream after the Town Lock was Child's Lock, at the point where the Botany Stream rejoins the main river. The lock was removed as part of the remodelling of the Navigation in the 1910s, but one wall of it remains in the south bank of the Medway. Stonework and parts of the wooden gate structures can be seen when the water is low.

H21 The Horsewash ●
NW. of the Big Bridge 590465

The Horsewash was the remains of part of the Castle moat forming a bay in the river some 10 yards wide, adjacent to the northwest corner of the Big Bridge, and accessible from the High Street (see picture on page 28). All and sundry could bring horses, carts, and even circus animals, there for a wash down. Access became difficult with the raising of the bridge approaches, and the Horsewash was removed in about 1900. The Watergate entrance to the Castle grounds now stands on the site.

H22 The New Cut ★
E. side of Racecourse Sportsground 588464

The New Cut is the first stretch dug for James Christie's Penshurst Canal in 1829, and formed a link between two branches of the Medway on the west side of the town. It is flanked on one side by the Racecourse sports ground and on the other by River Walk. The canal continued

H Transport

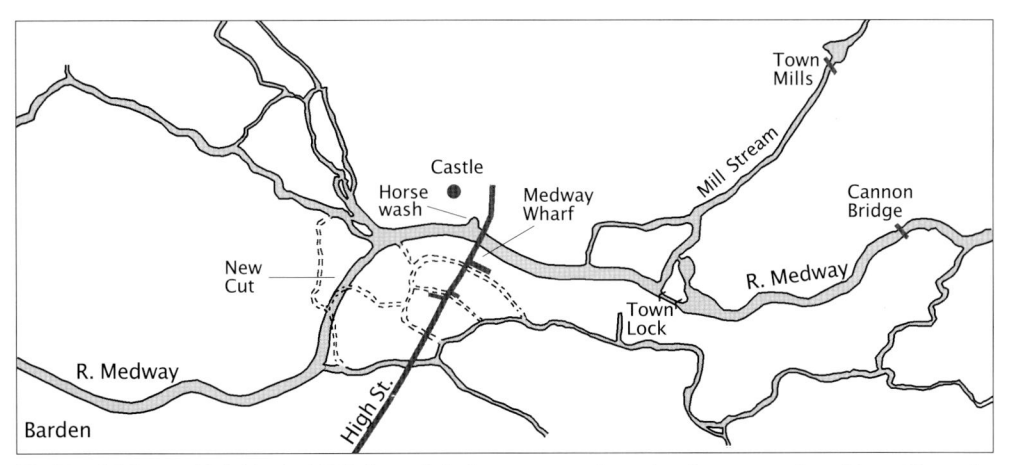

The River Medway at Tonbridge in 1871. Some of the lesser streams, shown dotted, are now culverted but still serve for storm water drainage.

along the straightened and improved stretch of river which runs parallel to Barden Road, and thence by the Long Reach to what is now Haysden Country Park.

H23   The Stone Lock   ★

Haysden Country Park   569460

The Stone Lock was constructed in about 1829 and is part of a section of James Christie's unfinished Penshurst Canal which would have straightened out a tortuous stretch of river known as The Shallows. The lock's stonework remains largely intact, though badly overgrown, and is usually dry except after heavy rain. It is Point 3 on the Historical Trail available at the car park in Haysden Country Park.

H24   The Straight Mile   ★

Haysden   566459 to 553456

The Straight Mile is a further section of Christie's Penshurst Canal which was dug in about 1830 but never filled. Its course remains clearly visible, except where obliterated by Haysden Water and the bypass, and can be followed by footpath. Some stonework is visible at the eastern end.

H25   Powder Mills canal   ★

Medway, near Barden Park   578466

By 1814 a canal had been cut to carry barges to and from the Powder Mills at Leigh (see B4). It branches from the north bank of the Medway on a bend opposite what is now Chestnut Walk. The canal has been cleared and is easily visible, including the abutments from a water-level control system. A number of footbridges in this area (e.g. at 57734672) were maintained by the Gunpowder Company, and appear to still have their original iron handrails.

H26   Riverside fortifications   ★

N. bank of the Medway, Barden area   57714661

Pillboxes were hurriedly built along the north side of the Medway in 1940, at a time when German invasion seemed imminent. Like Tonbridge Castle seven centuries earlier, their function was to deter, or at least delay, invaders from the south.

Among the boxes remaining in the area are three alongside the footpath on the north bank of the Long Reach near Lucifer Bridge: 57564645, 57714661 (shown here) and 57894671. All are Type 24 boxes, concrete, with small loopholes on five sides facing the river for the defenders to shoot from, and a sixth longer side with the entrance at the rear.

The Railway

The South Eastern Railway received assent for a line to Dover via Tonbridge in 1836. The route was to branch off the Brighton Line at Redhill (then called Reigate Junction) and would include a remarkable 46-mile stretch from Redhill to Ashford that is practically straight and almost level. Engineering works in the Tonbridge area included three encounters with the Medway at Haysden, cuttings at Leigh and Tudeley, and embankments between, together with new or realigned streets at the south end of the town.

By 1840 extra police were on duty in Tonbridge to deal with the influx of navvies. Materials such as rails and sleepers were delivered by barge to the Medway wharf, and the line was built from the Tonbridge end back to Redhill. It finally opened on 26th May 1842, but did not reach Dover until February 1844. Four trains ran daily each way between Tonbridge and London. The journey time for the 40-mile route was initially two hours, and a single second-class ticket cost 6s 6d, equivalent to £18 today. A branch to Tunbridge Wells was built to open in 1845 (H30), and included the Somerhill tunnel under Pembury Road and 30-arch Southborough viaduct.

Journey times from Tonbridge to London improved markedly with the opening of the direct route via Orpington, following the completion in 1868 of the Sevenoaks Tunnel – fifth longest in the country at the time – and relocation of the Tonbridge station (H31). Because of the need to give the Leigh Gunpowder Mills a wide berth, this route into Tonbridge was forced to take a sharp curve just north of the station which, though subsequently eased, has been a nuisance ever since. The line was not electrified until 1961.

With its routes to Sevenoaks, Redhill, Tunbridge Wells and Ashford, Tonbridge became the most important junction on the South Eastern (later South Eastern and Chatham) railway, complete with goods yard, cattle pens, engine sheds, and telegraph office (G3). 135 people worked for the railway in 1871, and in 1932 the Southern Railway (as it became in 1923) employed 650, making it the largest employer in the town.

The East Goods Yard in c.1870. The site of the original station is in the foreground. The 'new' station is in the distance. (THS 18/6)

The arrival of the railway changed the shape of Tonbridge, with a 'New Town' growing up south of the tracks as new streets were laid out and homes built.

H   Transport

The station entrance as it appeared from 1868 to 1934. (THS 18/46)

H27   First Railway Station   •
Between Vale and Priory Roads   589460

From 1842 to 1868 the original Tonbridge Station stood some 200 yards down the line from its present site. The up platform was reached along Priory Street, newly constructed for the purpose, with an entrance that is now the car park entrance opposite the British Legion Club, itself on the site of the former Telegraph Inn. The down platform was reached by Vale Road, which was improved for the purpose, at a point where the road narrows alongside the present Sainsbury filling station. The location of these two entrances can still be found but all trace of the station itself has gone. The engaving below shows it as a timber structure, with wooden bridge, stairs and platforms. The name was changed from Tunbridge to Tunbridge Junction in 1852.

Priory Street was so named to commemorate the ruined mediaeval priory which was obliterated by the railway-builders. Founded in 1124, the Priory stood in what is now the station car park nearest Vale Road and Station Approach, an area which later became the railway goods yard.

H28   Railway arches   ★
Railway Approach/Quarry Hill Road   587460

Before 1842, the main road to Tunbridge Wells followed a route along part of Barden Road and then along Waterloo Road towards Quarry Hill. It was originally planned that the railway would cross this turnpike by embankment and bridge, but plans changed and it was decided that a rerouted 'new turnpike' should cross the railway by an arched bridge on the line of the High Street, meeting up with the earlier route at the Brook Street junction. This was constructed in 1841, with four arches to carry the railway tracks and an additional foot tunnel on each side. The approach roads were built up using spoil from the railway cutting at Tudeley. The bridge was later broadened to form the new station entrance, but remains basically unchanged apart from the enlargement of the south foot tunnel to accommodate an additional track.

An engraving of the town's first railway station, which opened in 1842 – see H27. (THS 18/41)

H29 Medway Railway Viaduct ★
Haysden   560 460

For its chief engineer Mr (later Sir William) Cubitt, one of the most challenging sections of the South Eastern Railway to construct was in the vicinity of Leigh and Haysden. Three Medway crossings were required, all built in brick in c.1841, of which the most easterly consists of a six-arched viaduct, of which two arches span the river.

H30 Track of old railway ★
Near Goldsmid Road   593458

When the branch line to Tunbridge Wells opened in 1845 trains from Tonbridge had to back down the main line roughly to where the Sorting Office now is, and then run forward on a new line that curved up towards the Somerhill tunnel, Southborough viaduct and the Wells. This arrangement persisted until 1857 when the existing even steeper curve was built and reversing was no longer necessary. The original line remained in use for heavy goods trains until at least 1914, and its route can still be traced. Part of its embankment remains on the east side of Goldsmid Road, which it crossed by a narrow bridge, opposite Pembury Grove. It then ran up the east side of Pembury Grove, now re-landscaped as a grassed verge.

H31 The 'new' station ★
Railway Approach/Quarry Hill Road   587460

The present railway station on the west side of the road bridge was in place by the time the Sevenoaks route to London opened in 1868. Its name changed from Tunbridge Junction to Tonbridge Junction in 1893 and finally to Tonbridge in 1929. The cattle pens, yards and other sheds remained on the east side of the bridge with access from Vale Road, while the engine sheds were on the Priory Road side. A Post Office sorting office was added adjacent to the down side platform and Railway Approach and is part of the early station that still remains.

The original Victorian brickwork of the station entrance was replaced in 1934. At the same time £95,000 was spent on improve-

The 'new' station in 1888, with gas-lamps, engine water crane and top-hatted station-master. Platform 1, on the right, was still a bay at this time. (THS 18/5)

ments, including new signalling, re-alignment at the western end, and easing of the London curve. Later changes include more changes to the entrance, and further easing of the London curve for the benefit of the Channel Tunnel Eurostar trains that ran through Tonbridge from 1994 to 2003.

H32   Office of Colonel Stephens   ★

23 Salford Row   587459

In 1900, 23 Salford Row in Quarry Hill Road became the headquarters of the engineering practice of the colourful Colonel Holman Stephens (1868-1931), who engineered, built and managed an empire of 16 separate light or narrow gauge railways around the country. He also proposed many other railways that were not built, including the Hadlow Light Railway intended to carry farm produce down to Tonbridge. After his death the Salford Row offices remained headquarters of the practice until 1948. Furniture and other items from it are now displayed at the Tenterden Station of the revived Kent and East Sussex Railway which he built in 1900.

Principal Sources

Aaron, H., Pillar to Post – Looking at Street Furniture (Warne, 1982)
Austen, B., Tunbridge Ware and Related European Decorative Woodwares (Foulsham, 2001)
Barker-Read, M., *The Public Health question ...Tonbridge 1850-75*, Southern History, Vol. 4, 1982
Barty-King, H., Quiltwinders and podshavers: the history of cricket bat and ball manufacture (Macdonald and Jane's, 1979)
Brandon, P., Kent and Sussex Weald (Phillimore, 2003)
Chalklin, C.W., A Kentish Wealden Parish: Tonbridge 1550-1750, (Oxford B.Litt. Thesis)
Chalklin, C.W., *The Rural Economy of a Kentish Parish, 1650-1750*, Agricultural History Review, Vol. 10, 1962
Chalklin, C. W. (ed.), Early Victorian Tonbridge (Kent County Library, 1975)
Chalklin, C. W. (ed.), Mid-Victorian Tonbridge (Kent County Library, 1983)
Chalklin, C. W. (ed.), Late Victorian Tonbridge (Kent County Library, 1988)
Chalklin, C. W., *Sources for Kentish History: Trade and Industry*, Archaeologia Cantiana, Vol. 108, 1990
Chalklin, C. W. (ed.), Georgian Tonbridge (Tonbridge Historical Society, 1994)
Chalklin, C. W. (ed.), Tonbridge in the Early Twentieth Century (Tonbridge Historical Society, 1999)
Chalklin. C.W., *Iron Manufacture in Tonbridge Parish ...*, Archaeologia Cantiana, Vol. 124, 2004
Chapman, F., 'Ben Botany' weekly column in the Kent and Sussex Courier, 1963-72
Chapman, F., The Book of Tonbridge (Barracuda Books, 1976)
Chapman, F., Yesterday's Town: Tonbridge (Barracuda books, 1982)
Chapman, F., Tales of Old Tonbridge (Froglets, 1995)
Cleere, H., and Crossley, D., The Iron Industry of the Weald (Merton Priory Press, 1995)
Cuming, R., *The Mills of Tonbridge*, East Kent Mills Group Newsletter, 1986
Dendy Marshall, C. F., History of the Southern Railway (Ian Allan, 1963)
Dines, H. G. et al., Geology of the Country around Sevenoaks (H.M.S.O./Geol. Survey, 1969)
Directories, Local and County: including Pigot's, 1839, Post Office Directories, 1859 and 1874, and Kelly's, various dates to 1974
Egan, B., History of fire-fighting in Tonbridge, www.tonbridge-kent.com/Local-Inf/Pub-serv/fire/history.htm
Environment Agency, Medway Leap, Environmental Overview, 1999
Environment Agency, The Leigh Barrier (no date)

Eve, D., Guide to the Industrial Archaeology of Kent (Association for Industrial Archaeology, 1999)
Gill, M. A. V., Tunbridge Ware (Shire Publications, 1985)
Guides: Official Guides to Tonbridge, various dates
Hoole, G. P., A Tonbridge Miscellany (privately printed, 1985)
Institute of Quarrying, Archive Sources (no date)
Maps: Ordnance Survey maps, all editions 1866 to present; Tithe Map 1838 and Apportionment 1841
Melling, E., (ed.), Kentish Sources I – Some Roads and Bridges (Kent County Council, 1959)
Melling, E., (ed.), Kentish Sources III – Aspects of Agriculture and Industry (Kent County Council, 1961)
Neve, A. H., The Tonbridge of Yesterday (Tonbridge Free Press, 1933)
Newspapers: Tonbridge Free Press 1871-1964, Kent and Sussex Courier 1873 to present
Preston, J. M., Industrial Medway (J. M. Preston, 1977)
Rivington, S., The History of Tonbridge School (Rivingtons, 1910)
Science Museum Library, The Simmons Collection – archive material, 1974
Skinner, D., Old Tonbridge (Meresborough Books, 1981)
Tapsell, M., Memories of Kent Cinemas (Plateway, Croydon, 1987)
Thirsk, J., *Agriculture in Kent, 1540-1640*, in Zell, M. (ed.), Early Modern Kent, 1540-1640 (Boydell Press/KCC, 2000)
Tonbridge School, Local History Research Papers, 1969
Victoria County History, Kent, Vol. 3 (St. Catherine Press, 1932)
Vince, J., Fire-Marks (Shire Publications, 1989)
Wealden Iron Research Group, Bulletins, various dates
West Kent Water Company, Your Water Supply, 1976

List of Subscribers

Presentation Copies

The President of Tonbridge Historical Society, Miss Stella Hardy, MBE

The Mayor of Tonbridge and Malling, Councillor Derek Still

The Editor and Contributors

Subscribers

Mr & Mrs John Adams
Susan J. Adams
Mr & Mrs R. G. Allibone
Ken Archer
Jean Ashton
Mr & Mrs R. E. Austin
Mrs C. M. Baldock
Audrey Barber
Rosemary Barton
Betty Batchelor
Mrs Jane Beach
Neil & Rosie Benfield
Pam Benstead
Miss Barbara Bentall
Mary Bickmore
Frank G. Blundell
Marjorie Blundell
Dr R. F. Bolam
John Boulding
Clare & Stan Bowerman
Stephen Briggs
Mr & Mrs C. Bristow
Jean & Allan Broadbent
Shiela & Chris Broomfield
Peter & Yvonne Burgess
Wendy Burton
Margaret Carr
Jack & Betty Carter
James & Sylvia Carter
Geoffrey Cash
Andrew & Dorothy Chalklin
Christopher & Mavis Chalklin
Mrs J. Challis
Ronald Church

Mr & Mrs R. Churchman
Dr C. H. & Mrs P. M. Collins
Ian Coulson
P. M. Cracknell
Mr P. R. Cripps
Marie Cross
Mr & Mrs A. K. Dane
Jill Davison
Miss J. M. Debney
Thelma Dillistone
John F. Dorling
Chris Easeman
David W. M. Easton
Mr Gerald Ellard
Mr J. G. Ellis
Mr A. J. & Mrs C. H. Everest
Ray Everett
Elizabeth Finn
Dr & Mrs J. M. T. Ford
Flora Fowles
Mrs M. Fraser
Mr & Mrs C. J. F. Gardner
Martin Garwood
Ian Goodacre
Mrs E.J. Hamman
Keith Hammond & Joyce Hammond
Mrs Mabel Hammond
Anthony & Annabelle Hayward
Mr & Mrs R. J. Hedley-Jones
Kevin & Irene Hemsley
Guy Hitchings
Mr John Hoath
Brenda Hook
Rebecca & Darrell Howard

Anne Hughes
Dr P. L. Humphries
Diane M. Huntingford
Philip Hurling
John Irving
Maureen Jackson
Abby Jeffery
Shaun Jeffery
Mrs William Jenner
Roger Joye
KCC Libraries & Archives
Mr & Mrs David Kemp
Mr & Mrs G. J. Kemp
J. King
Claire Knight
Mr R. Large
Mr P. S. Leach
Pauline & Nick Luck
A. W. & D. R. Mankelow
Ron Martin
Mr & Mrs David Marwood
Mr & Mrs J. McAuslan
Mrs Richard McKay
Roger Millman
Anne Mills
Mr & Mrs D. R. Mitchell
Heather & Callum Morgan
Mr & Mrs N. J. Moss
Michael Norrie
Andrew J. Paulson
James Pavlidis
John Pavlidis
Margaret Pavlidis
Derek & Barbara Payne
Michael Pead
David Penny
Michael Penny
Margaret & Denis Pidgeon
Mr & Mrs Timothy Pierce
M. Pollard
Mr & Mrs A. M. Porteous
John & Sally Potter
Reg Potts
Eleanor Prentis
Brian Price
Paula Rangecroft
Dr John Ray

Jonathan & Stella Ripley
Dr & Mrs S. N. Robbins
Mr & Mrs D. M. Robins
Abi S. Saunders
Andrew J. O. Saunders
Andrew O. W. Saunders
Jake A. O. Saunders
Melanie C. Saunders
Neil C. Saunders
Susan A. Saunders
Cllr Miss Janet Sergison
Joy Shaw
Margaret & Neil Shilling
Mr & Mrs S. Simmons
Tom Simmons
Paul Sinclair
Mr & Mrs E. J. Smalman-Smith
Geoffrey Smethurst
Mrs Mary Smith
Mike Smith
Sonia & Chris Smith
John Stevens
Peter & Chris Stibbard
Joan Thirsk
Nicholas Thompson
Mrs G .W. Todd
Tonbridge Civic Society
Tonbridge Library
Nigel & Eva Trippett
Muriel Trumper
Junia & Eric Wadsworth
Mr & Mrs G. Wallwork
Mrs Ellen Ware
Mr William Ware
Philip Waterhouse
Mr & Mrs Don & Margaret Webster
John Weston
Helen Wheeler
Peter Wildbur
Richard Willey
Alison Williams
Don Wilson
Sarah Wilson
Mr & Mrs T. N. Wilson
Mollie Woodrow
M. E. Woods
George Young

Index

Acme Chemical Company 57
Agriculture 23–26
Allen family, blacksmiths 48, 49
Angel Ground 80

Baker family, brewers 28
Barr, Lamb Ltd 60
Bartram family, brewers 28
Bench mark 86
Blacksmiths 47–48
Boundary posts 85–86
Bradbury and Agnew 55–56
Breweries 27–28
    Bridge 27
    Quarry Hill 28
Brick and tile making sites 15, 40–45
Brickfields and brickworks 41–45
    Castle Hill 43–44
    Haysden 44
    Lavender Hill 43
    London Road 44
    Pittswood 45
    Priory Road 43
    Punnett's 41
    Quarry Hill 42–43
    Shipbourne Road E. and W. 44–45
    Starvecrow 45
    Vauxhall 43
Bridges
    Big (Great) Bridge 28, 83
    Cannon Lane 57, 84
    Little (Lower) Bridge 83
    Medway Viaducts 84, 92
    Sutton's 83
British Berkefeld Filters 58–59
British Flint and Cerium Manfrs 60
British Resin Products 60
Brown, Knight and Truscott 56
Burton, James 35
Bypass 84

Castle 17, 38–39, 69, 87, 88
Castle Valves 66
Cattle Market 31
Chalklin family 43, 45, 58
Charlton, J. S., mill-owner 33, 88
Children, George 35
Christie, James 33, 87, 88, 89

Cinemas 78–79
    Capitol 79
    Central Picture Hall 79
    Empire Picture Palace 79
    Pavilion 79
    Ritz 79
    Star 79
Cloth trade, Wealden 26
Clothiers 26
Coal hole cover 86
Communications and entertainment 74–80
Corn Exchange 31
Coules family, blacksmiths 47
Cowcheman family, clothiers 26
Cricket ball factories 51–53
    Smith and Ives/Wisden 52–53
    Thomas Ives 53
Crystalate Company 53, 57–58
Cutlery industry 47

Davy, Sir Humphry 35
Distiller's Company 60
Doust Brothers, hop and seed factors 30
Drinking fountain and troughs 84, 85
Drury family, blacksmiths 48

E.C.D. Ltd 59–60
Electricity supply 69–71
    Electric Light Station 69, 71
    pillar and switch boxes 71
    Somerhill generating station 71
Engineering works
    Allen/Welch 49
    Goodland 49, 59
Extractive industry 15, 38–46

Farms and oasts 24–26
    Bourne 25
    Brook Street 24, 25
    Cage 25–26
    Cage Green 26
    Dry Hill 26
    Hilden 25
    Peach Hall 24
    Postern Park 23
    Pot Kiln 25
    Priory 24
    Starvecrow 26

Farms and oasts *ctd.*
   Tanyard 27
   Tilehouse 24
Fire
   hooks 72
   hydrant cover 72
   hydrant indicator 72–73
   insurance marks 72
   Station 73
Flood Control Barrier 68–69
Flooding 66–67
Foundries
   Gray Brothers 47, 48–49
   Seale, Austen and Barnes 48, 71, 82, 86

Gas supply 62–64
   gasworks 62
   forge 63
   gasholders 63
   Somerhill 64
Goodland family, engineers 49, 59
Gravel wells 66
Gravel working sites 15
   Ballast Pit 46
   Barden Lake 46
   Hawden 46
   Haysden Water 46
   Postern area 46
Gray Brothers 47, 48–49
Gunpowder 34–36

Harman, Anthony, brewer 27–28
Hooker, John 87
Hop-growing 23, 24, 30. *See also* Farms and oasts
Horsewash 28, 88
Humphrey Bean pub 30, 75

Industrial estate 57–61
Inns 27–30
   Angel 29
   Bull 28–29
   Castle 30, 88
   Chequers 29
   Dorset Arms 30
   George and Dragon 30
   Loggerheads 30
   Red Lion 29
   Rose and Crown 28
Iron industry, Wealden 16, 32–33, 36–37, 38
   Bourne Mill furnace 36
   Postern forge 36
   Rat's Castle bloomery 37
   Vauxhall furnace 36
Ives, Thomas, cricket ball maker 51, 52-53

Jewhurst family, mill-owners 33

Lillywhite Frowd 52
Local Board 64, 67–68, 72
Locks 87–89
   Child's lock 88
   Stone lock 89
   Town lock 88
Lyons Wharf 88

Manufacturing industry 50–61
Maps of sites 8–9, 13, 15
Market 30–31, 86
Maylam's Quay 88
Medway Hall 80
Medway Navigation Company 86–87
Medway, River 32, 86–89
   New Cut 88–89
   Straight Mile 89
Medway Wharf 87, 88
Metalworking and engineering 47–49
Mileplate 84
Mills 32–37. *See also* iron industry, Wealden
   Bourne Mill 34
   Cage Green windmill 37
   Leigh Powdermills 34–36
   Priory Mill 34
   Ramhurst Mill 36
   Town Mills 33–34
Mortley Sprague and Co. 59

Oasts 25. *See also* Farms and oasts
Omnibus depot 49

Parish Church 18, 30, 41, 62, 72
Penshurst Canal 87, 88, 89
Pillboxes 89
Postal service 74–75
   post box 75
   post office 74, 75, 76
Powdermills, Leigh 34–36, 90
   canal 89
Power station. *See* Electricity supply
Printers
   Blair 20, 54
   Bridger 53, 54
   Dowgate Press (Brown, Knight and Truscott) 56
   Stonestreet 54
   Tonbridge Printers 56
   Ware 54, 80
   Whitefriars Press (Bradbury, Agnew) 55–56
Printing industry 53–56
Public Hall 79
Pump, public 28, 64
Punnett family, builders etc., 41

Index

Quarrying sites 15, 38–40

Racecourse Sportsground 80
Railway, South Eastern 75, 90–93
   arches 91
   first station 91
   Hadlow light railway 93
   Medway viaduct 92
   'new' station 91, 92
   track of old railway 92
Recreation 78–80
Reeve, Giles, bell-founder 47
Reservoirs
   Bloodshots 65
   Hangman's Hill 66
   Kilnwood 65
Roads 17, 81–83
   High Street 82
   old Rye road 83
   Roman trackway 82–83
   turnpikes 81
Roadside shelter 85

Seale, Austen and Barnes 48, 71, 82, 86
Sewage 67–68
   ejector 68
   pumping station 68
   works 68
Sheepskin Utilities 60
Skating rink 80
Slack and Brownlow 58–59
Smith, Charles, cricket ball maker 51, 52, 53
Smithies
   Coules 47
   Drury/Allen 48
   Waghorn 47
Somerhill 64, 71, 83
South-Eastern Tar Distillers (SETAR) 59
Sportsground 80
Stagg, Rowland, fellmonger 27
Stephens, Col. H. 93
Stonestreet, Manasseh, printer etc. 54
Storey Motor Company 34, 58
Straight Mile 89
Street furniture 84–86
Street lamp, electric 71
Surface drainage and sewerage 66–68

Tannery 27
Telegraph service 75–77
   telegraph office 74, 77

Telephone service 75–76, 77
   footway box cover 77
   G.P.O. service indicator 77
   National company 76
   South of England company 76
   telephone box 77
   telephone exchange 76, 77
Tollgate marker 84
Tonbridge
   geology 15–16
   history 17–22
   population 17, 18, 19, 20, 21
   relief and drainage 13–14
   topography 13–14, 17
Tonbridge Cricket Club 80
Tonbridge Football Club 80
Tonbridge Free Press 54
Tonbridge Gas Company 62–63
Tonbridge Printers 56
Tonbridge School 21, 28, 41, 62, 63, 78, 85
Tonbridge Stock and Cattle Market Co. 31, 86
Town Wardens 64, 67, 85
Transport 81–93
Tunbridge Ware 50–51
Tyler, E.W., and Co. 61

Uridge brothers, millers 37
Utilities and services 62–73

Vestry, Parish 18, 19, 67, 72

Walker, Charles V. 75, 76
Wallace and Tiernan 34, 59–60
Ware family, printers etc. 54, 74, 80
Water and wind power 13, 32–37
   See also mills
Water supply 64–66
   reservoirs 65–66
   stopcock covers 66
   water works 65
Welch family, engineers 49
Weller family 29
West, 'Buster' 79
Whitefriars Press 55–56
Wightwick, Humphrey, tallow chandler 88
Willard, Davy, ironmaster 36
Wisden, John, cricket ball maker 51, 52, 53
Wise family 28, 49, 51, 85
Wise's Manufactory 51
Woolstapler and fellmonger 27